Pugs

The Owner's Guide from Puppy to Old Age

Choosing, Caring for, Grooming, Health, Training
and Understanding Your Pug Dog or Puppy

By Alex Seymour

Copyright and Trademarks

ISBN: 978-1-910677-08-7. Copyright © 2018 by Dog Experts Publishing. For comments, questions, requests for review copies and bulk order discounts please email: help@feelhappybooks.com

Disclaimer and Legal Notice

Foreword

Congratulations on purchasing this book. You've made a wise choice, as many of the world's top Pug breeders have been involved in contributing to this book.

Once you've reached the end, you will have all the information you need to make a well-informed decision whether or not the Pug is the breed for you. **Also, at the end, you will find a very special surprise in store as a thank-you for buying this book!**

As an expert trainer and professional dog whisperer, I will teach you the human side of the equation, so you can learn how to think more like your Pug and eliminate behavioral problems.

Here is how I first met (and fell in love with) the Pug…

Bentley had a face straight out of a gangster movie. I swear if you had given that dog a cigar and a fedora he would have been a dead ringer for Edward G. Robinson. The first time I met him, the Pug began circling my chair, muttering dark canine trash talk under his breath.

"What am I doing wrong?" I asked Bentley's owner.

"You're sitting in his chair," my friend Mike said, reaching for a sticky roller. "And you're going to be covered in dog hair."

My friend Mike, injured early in life in a car accident, had limited mobility, but loved dogs. He was attracted to Pugs as a breed because they have reasonably low exercise needs. Mike had a fenced backyard, and Bentley was good going out a couple of times a day to play. The rest of the time he could be found snoring in his bed under Mike's desk.

Beyond the shedding, Mike related absolute horrors of housebreaking lessons that went on for six months. "I thought I'd lose my mind," Mike said. "But once he got it we were good. Until it rains. Mr. Precious Paws there doesn't like to get his feet wet."

At that, Bentley let out a rather undignified and world weary moan and we both laughed. At that sound, the dog perked up, fixed us with a quizzical look and Mike said, "Go get your toy, little man."

Bentley played with the same degree of enthusiasm he brought to napping and was one of the funniest dogs I think I've ever seen. I fell in love with him and asked if I could bring him treats next time I came over.

"One treat," Mike warned. "He's a chow hound and I have to watch him so he doesn't get too fat. And I'm warning you. If you show up with a treat once, he'll expect you to bring him something every time."

Mike was right. As soon as Bentley saw me come in the door, he was an absolute pest until I handed out his "surprise," usually a Greenies dental chew which seemed to be the best healthy compromise.

When Mike had to go into the hospital for hip replacement surgery, he asked me if I'd take Bentley until he was home and could at least get around well enough to let the dog out. I was happy to do it, and was surprised by how well Bentley started running my household.

One of the dog's favorite daily "chores" was the cleaning of his facial wrinkles. He all but hummed with pleasure as I used a baby wipe to clean out the creases on his face and dry them with gauze. He slept with me, and snored like a buzz saw, but darned if he didn't look so comfortable, I didn't mind.

When I took him home, Bentley seemed to immediately understand that Mike was under the weather, and was great about not getting in the way of the crutches or otherwise tripping up his lame human. Later Mike admitted that getting over the hip replacement was so hard, he didn't think he would have gotten through it without Bentley making him laugh.

They were together for 14 years before Bentley passed of old-age related illnesses. He was a very healthy dog until the last six months of his life and after a decent mourning period, Mike called to tell me he

had a Pug puppy. I went over to meet the new dog and was greeted by a whirling dervish of a dog that seemed to stop and pee on the carpet every five minutes.

Photo Credit: Jane Dowdy of Goneroamin Pugs.

"How are you doing with having a young dog in the house?" I asked Mike, who looked like he'd been through armed combat.

"Well, I'm definitely not as young as I was when I did this last time," he said, "but what can I say? Bentley ruined me for any other breed."

It's a common sentiment among Pug owners. As you will read in this book, the dogs are not without their challenges, but they are one of the most popular toy companion breeds for good reason — they have the companion part of the equation nailed and they're great fun!

Acknowledgments

In writing this book, I also sought tips, advice, photos, and opinions from many worldwide experts on the Pug breed including influential members of the Pug Dog Clubs of America, Canada, UK and Australia. In particular, I wish to thank the following wonderful breeders and vets for their outstanding help and contributions:

United States Contributors

H. Michael Anderson and Michelle Anderson of SandCastlePugs
Email: SandCastlePugs@sc.rr.com

Christine Dresser DVM, Health Liaison, Pug Dog Club of America

Vallarie Smith Cuttie of Peachtree Pugs
Email: vallarie@cuttie.com

David Johnson (DVM) and Judith Johnson (CVT) of Foursquare Pugs
Email: baileybuttonboy@yahoo.com

Pam Donaldson of Highland/Kendoric Pugs
Email: PhdPugs@Comcast.net

Dr. Jeff and Amy McLelland of Pickwick Pugs
http://www.PickwickPugs.com

Laura Libner of Lorarlar Pugs
Email: loralarpugluv@gmail.com

Julianne McCoy of Low Country Pugs
Email: juliannemccoy2409@comcast.net

Christina Hedrick and Cathleen Codling of Wahoo Pugs & Pug Rescue of North Carolina, Inc
http://www.wahoopugs.com

Connie J. Dunham of MtnAire Pugs
http://mtnairepugs.com/

Acknowledgments

Doris Klingbeil of Gibby Pugs
http://www.gibbypugs.com

Brenda Shellehamer of Brendy Pugs
http://www.BrendyPugs.com

Rosemary Robles of Pocket Pugs
http://www.pocket-pugs.com/

Jade Hall of SmugPugs
Email: Jade.SmugPugs@Gmail.com

Jeanne Hilton Henderson of Hilton Kennels
Email: moddog@msn.com

Annie Sullivan of CASull Pugs
http://casullpugs.com

Michele Bearden of Charmin Pugs
http://charmindogs.com

Patrick Archer McManus—Pug show judge

Christina Givens of Wind Valley Pugs
http://windvalleypugs.org/

Steve and Debbie Baldwin of Enchanted Pugs
Email: enchantedpugs@comcast.net

Jim Bradley of Joie De Vivre Pugs
Email: yoyogator@msn.com

United Kingdom Contributors

Julia Ashton of Zobear Pugs
http://www.zobearpugs.co.uk

Sue Lee of Tsuselena Pugs
http://tsuselena.com/

Hilary Linnett of Conquell Pugs
http://www.conquellpugs.co.uk/

Gail Saffer of Ragemma Pugs
http://www.ragemmapug.com/

Julie Squire and Holly Attwood of Taftazini
Email: taftazini@hotmail.co.uk

Australia

Felicity Prideaux of Hugapug
http://www.hugapug.com.au

Belinda Goyarts of Raevon Pugs
http://www.raevonpugs.com/

Jane Dowdy of Goneroamin Pugs
Email: goneroamin@skymesh.com.au

Judy Horton—Pug show judge.

Canada

Tannis Postma of Pekeapug Kennels
http://www.pekeapug.com/

Michelle Chisholm of Siosalach Pugs
http://www.siosalachshar-pei.com

Jenny Duffy of Kalmadray Pugs
http://www.freewebs.com/kalamad/

Heidi Merkli of Bugaboo Reg'd
http://www.bugaboodogs.ca

Lorna Sale of Poohpugs Perm. Reg.
Email: poohpugs@gmail.com

James and Mary Lou Dymond of Jimary Pugs
http://www.jimarypugs.com/

Lundi Blamey of Claripugs
Email: lundi1000@gmail.com

Special thanks to photographer Wendy Davenschot of Viking Mops,
Pugtography (see her gorgeous photo below):
http://www.vikingmops.com

When the world around
me is going crazy and
I am losing faith in
humanity, I just have
to take one look at
my Pug to know that...

Good still exists

**FANCY SOME PUG FUN? WE ALSO RECOMMEND DOGS GO
AROUND THE WORLD BY FEEL HAPPY
COLOURING BOOKS...**

This top-selling coloring book aimed at adults
and older children has a page on the Pug (as
well as 24 other popular dog breeds).

Available on Amazon and other good online
bookstores, this is a memorable gift idea for
relaxation, fun, and enjoyment.

Table of Contents

Table of Contents

Table of Contents

Chapter 1 — Meet the Pug

The Pug is a wonderful combination of comedian and dignified companion. A dog that thrives in the company of his humans, the Pug is always up for a game, ready to dispense affection, or seek the center of attention—generally all at one time! Ignore a Pug, and you'll have a very unhappy (and insistent) little dog on your hands.

Some experts think the name "Pug" comes from the Latin for "fist," which may be a reference to the shape of the breed's face. Others claim the name is derived from the old word for goblin or small monkey. An alternate, but unofficial explanation could be the way these dogs punch through all barriers of inattention and make sure they aren't just noticed, but included in everything that's going on!

The purpose of this book is to consider Pugs as family pets. In the United States, they are currently the 32nd most popular breed based on registration numbers at the American Kennel Club (AKC). The UK Kennel Club has them even higher as the 4th most popular breed.

Compared to other breeds Pugs have a unique look and personality which is why they are so popular. It's hard to look at a Pug smiling up at you and not smile back. The breed has a friendly, open demeanor accentuated by the dog's dark facial coloration (mask), deep-set wrinkles, short nose, dark eyes, and generally moderate underbite. The look is in keeping with the Pug's reputation for being a canine clown, renowned for his love of showing off.

Pugs are **easy enough to maintain** in terms of grooming requiring perhaps 30 minutes to an hour each week, although they do shed their coats all through the year with peak periods in spring and fall (autumn). On a weekly basis, you should brush their coat once or twice, keep their faces clean and check their eyes daily for problems. Once a month you will need to trim their toe nails and give them a bath.

Pugs are also **easy in terms of exercise**, of course they love walks as much as the next dog but there are other higher activity breeds if that is what you are looking for. In addition you should be aware that being a short-nosed breed they can **easily become overheated** and have difficulty in high temperatures.

While Pugs are very amiable, playful and confident dogs they **can certainly be stubborn** too, which makes for a challenge when it comes to training them!

Pugs are an extremely brachycephalic (flat-faced) breed and can suffer from breathing difficulties, eye problems and skin problems. While it is important to be aware of these issues before you buy one, these needn't put you off as the thousands of Pug owners worldwide will tell you. At an **average lifespan prediction of 15 years** on the far side, Pugs are long-lived little dogs.

You'll often see the Pug described as, "multum in parvo." It's an apt description since it basically means, "big dog in a little body." Pugs are a member of the Toy breed group, these small companion dogs are commonly referred to as "lapdogs". Most toy breeds love attention and are very friendly and affectionate. Pugs make a **great choice for both young (families) and old alike**. They love being with their owners and don't like being left alone for long periods of time.

Experienced Pug breeders from all over the world have kindly given their time to answer questions and give their expert advice. You are about to benefit from literally hundreds of years' experience of living with Pugs and breeding them.

Amy McLelland of Pickwick Pugs tells us the best things about the Pug: "My husband Jeff and I chose this breed when we first married after scouring through a dog breed book. Initially, we were attracted to the book's statement that they required minimal grooming and exercise and loved to sit on laps.

"After spending 27 years living with this breed, I can now say that what I love most about Pugs is their playful personalities and loving dispositions. Pugs are intelligent little clowns, packed with personality, and can get under your skin with their funny antics and sometimes independent minds. Bred specifically for companionship, Pugs are very social creatures and thrive when they are with their "people", whether humans or other playmate, (preferably another Pug)."

Christina Hedrick and Cathleen Codling of Wahoo Pugs & Pug Rescue of North Carolina, Inc on why choose a Pug compared to other breeds: "I think people become addicted to Pugs because of their funny, outgoing personalities. They want to be with their human so if you go to the bathroom you are sure to have someone in tow. This makes the breed special to me. Pugs are not a yappy dog like most of your toy breeds and are often referred to as a big dog in a small body. They love nothing more than to please you. All these qualities are why I think Pugs are a special breed and stand out from the rest."

Physical Size and Appearance

For this section we wish to sincerely thank **Judy Horton** who judges Pugs in the show ring for kindly supplying illustrations and comments.

The modern Pug is a compact, cobby dog with a squarish body, a deep chest, and well-developed musculature. It stands on moderately long, straight legs that are strong and set well under the body. The small feet are an oval shape with thick pads and clearly defined toes sporting black nails. Rear feet are slightly smaller than the front.

The head is large, exceptionally so in relation to the rest of the body, and round. Indentations of any kind or an "apple" head are undesirable. The head should have a very short and well developed square foreface without the slightest sign of "turn up" of the nose. The head has a distinctively round shape yet the top of the skull is relatively flat.

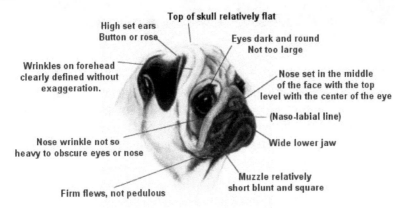

Top of skull relatively flat

High set ears
Button or rose

Eyes dark and round
Not too large

Wrinkles on forehead
clearly defined without
exaggeration.

Nose set in the middle
of the face with the top
level with the center of the eye

(Naso-labial line)

Nose wrinkle not so
heavy to obscure eyes or nose

Wide lower jaw

Firm flews, not pedulous

Muzzle relatively
short blunt and square

Head wrinkles are important to give the breed its typical expression. The wrinkles on the forehead are deep and in a fan shape and they are set off by the darkening of the folds. The surplus skin under the throat and around the face forms a large fold or ruff. The wrinkles on the forehead come together in a diamond shape sometimes called a thumb mark which is seen in fawn dogs.

The black nose is set in the center of the face, the top of the nose being on a level with the center of the eyes. The nose must have well opened nostrils. Viewed from the side the muzzle should be as short and flat as possible and from the front it should be wide and well filled up under the eyes and almost equal to the width of the forehead.

The neck should be slightly arched to resemble a strong, thick crest, with enough length to carry the head proudly. The neck should increase in breadth as it blends smoothly into the well-placed shoulders.

Julianne McCoy of Low Country Pugs: "Pugs can be pretty smart. One thing we talk about is once a Pug matures, their head should pop (get larger) and their chest should drop forcing them to walk correctly with their legs apart. You should see a square when you look at a Pug from any angle."

Rose ear   Button ear

Pugs have two ear types: rose and button. Of the two, the rose ear is rounder and smaller, folding so that the front edge sits against the side of the head. The preference for breeding and show purposes, however, is the larger button ear, which sits level with the top of the forehead and folds at a precise 90-degree angle. The thin, small ears set high and to the outside are velvet soft.

The eyes should be prominent, bold, and dark, but full of fire and mischief when the dog is excited. Color should be dark brown or black and is unaffected by coat color. These large, dark eyes should be set well apart with black rims and in fawn dogs surrounded by a dark mask.

The mask is the black coloring of the muzzle and is part of what gives the Pug its unique appearance. It starts under the chin and covers the entire muzzle, rises over the top of the nose and then encircles both eyes.

The trace is the straight line running down the Pug's back. Don't worry, this is considered to be an official marking of the breed and is not a disqualification if you wish to show your Pug. The trace is not always present and is highly prized. It should be a fine shading of dark hair from occiput to tail along the spine.

We asked **Jane Dowdy of Goneroamin Pugs** if potential new owners come to her with misconceptions or myths about Pugs: "Many potential puppy buyers ask me if it is true that their eyes can just pop out. Yes Pug's eyes do have the potential to "pop out" but it rarely happens and is usually due to a traumatic injury or result of a fight with another Pug. I stress to new owners the importance of knowing how their Pug's eyes look normally. Any variation from the norm such as squinting or bluish tinge to the eye means it is then very important to get the Pug to the vet as soon as possible. Early treatment is essential for a good outcome."

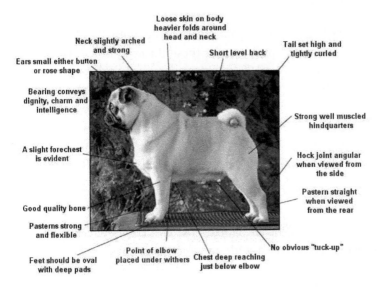

Rosemary Robles of Pocket Pugs says: "Most prospect buyers are interested in getting the correct size of the Pug. The standard is 14–18 pounds for the USA and we are in the toy group. They want to be able to travel with their Pugs on the plane and in the cabin with them. The Pug was bred for companionship and wants to be with you at all times. Size is important since they most likely will be carrying him or her or having them on their laps. All Pugs have great personalities, very clown like and entertaining."

We asked Australian breeder Felicity Prideaux of Hugapug if Pugs in Australia are any different to those in the US and the UK.

"With the ability to ship semen and import dogs I think that the difference between Pugs in the various countries is blurring. My preference has always been for the American style over the English style, simply because to me they are consistently square in outline and demonstrate, what I believe is, the correct length of leg. Over the years I've seen many videos of Pugs in the UK who are long in back and shorter in leg than I like to see. However more recent videos from the UK are showing many dogs displaying an outline that I prefer."

On average, Pugs stand 12–14 in. / 30.48–35.56 cm. at the shoulder and weigh 14–18 lb. / 6.35-8.16 kg.

Know from the beginning of your relationship with this breed that **obesity can be a serious problem** for these thickset little dogs, so it's quite common to see 20 lb. / 9.07 kg. Pugs, even though that may not be the healthiest body weight for the breed. One of the biggest contributors to longevity is not to fall for the big pleading eyes that demand food! Sadly, many older Pugs are overweight, which leads to issues with joints, heart, and skin. The excess fat can produce chemicals that speed up joint deterioration. The fittest Pugs live the longest!

Coat, Color, Tail

The American Kennel Club recognizes just two colors which are fawn and black. Fawn can cover a wide range of hues that vary from very light fawn to a darker fawn that is similar to tan. A silver or apricot Pug will be registered as a fawn.

The FCI (World Canine Organization) and Kennel Club in the UK allows for four colors for the Pug: silver, apricot, fawn or black.

The Canadian Kennel Club (CKC) allows for 3 colors: fawn, silver-fawn or black (fawn can be any shade from light apricot, deep apricot to reddish gold.

To date science has conclusively proven that the naturally occurring colours in Pugs are black and shades in the fawn spectrum, those being fawn, apricot and silver. All Pugs also carry the gene which creates the wonderful black mask and ear colouring. So, what if your Pug is brindle or all white or pied or black and tan? This simply means that one of your Pug's ancestors was crossed with another breed, such as a Boston Terrier, French Bulldog, Staffordshire Bull Terrier or Griffon in order to introduce these new colours. These colours are not recognised by any kennel club, but that doesn't stop your Pug being your best friend and an amazing companion.

The solid black Pug without any other markings is one of the rarest coat colors as they usually have an additional color known as a marking.

Julianne McCoy of Low Country Pugs: "One issue we are having with the Pugs is that we have some breeders that are not breeding appropriately. They are breeding the Pug to a Boston Terrier or back to a French Bulldog to get a brindle Pug. There is no such thing as a brindle Pug. These dogs are mixed breeds."

Photo Credit: Felicity Prideaux of Hugapug and Wilomark Imagery.
Single coat on left and double on right.

David and Judith Johnson of Foursquare Pugs: "We are fighting a battle here in the States with those that would genetically hurt our breed by not health testing, or breeding mixed breeds, or breeding unrecognized colors. White, blue or brindle colors are totally unacceptable under the breed standard. These dogs are being sold for a lot of money as rare. They are not rare, they are mixed breeds."

Felicity Prideaux of Hugapug: "Pups do change colour as they age, winter coats are often a different shade than summer coats. Blacks, particularly if born from a black and a fawn parent, show a reddish tinge to their coat as the old coat starts to fall out and new coat comes through. Blacks can be both single and double coated. As fawns and blacks were bred together, so the double black coat began to be more common."

Pam Donaldson of Highland/Kendoric Pugs: "There are other countries that do not prefer the double coat that we prefer in the US. The US Pugs do have a tendency to be fluffy coated and very soft to touch. Fawn Pug puppies are born quite dark and may even exhibit some stripe like patterns for the first couple days after birth. Over the weeks, they gradually lighten usually from the legs up. Black puppies are always black but they may also have degrees of blackness depending how much fawn genetics is in their background. Some blacks may even have few fawn hairs mixed in their coats, which isn't desirable in a show dog, but they are still black; not silver or blue.

"Fawn and black Pugs often have white markings on their chests which are quite evident on a black Pug, but not easily seen on a light coated fawn. The white mark on a black show Pug's chest is supposed to be small and in some countries not acceptable in the show ring at all. Judging results often seem to indicate a preference for the fawn color. I have been told that it can be hard for judges to see the expression on a black Pug's face and I have been told dog photographers prefer fawn Pugs for this same reason."

Sue Lee of Tsuselena Pugs: "The Pugs from abroad are easy to spot in the UK show ring and as enthusiasts we should be able to celebrate the differences. The dogs we see from other countries do have slightly longer legs and I think better bone and forward reach. The UK Pugs generally have a less 'stuffy' neck with more of a crest. There are excellent examples to be seen from different countries albeit with slightly different Breed Standards.

"The biggest easily visible difference is the Pug coat. UK Pug's coats are naturally short and untrimmed. The UK Breed Standard is very clear that coats must not be clipped, stripped or scissored. Our Breed Specialist judges would consider a longer coat as any other fault or departure from the Breed Standard."

The Pug's tail, which is relatively short, stands up over the hip in a curl. There are various "sets" to describe the tail position including:

- high and tight with a double curl
- single curl
- set overly high above the back
- hanging loose with no curl
- set low but close to the body

The AKC breed standard, in reference to the tail reads, "The short back is level from the withers to the high tail set. The body is short and cobby, wide in chest and well ribbed up. The tail is curled as tightly as possible over the hip. The double curl is perfection."

Pug Health Issues

Brachycephalic means "shortened" head and refers to the short nose and flat face of dogs like Pugs, Shih Tzus, Chihuahuas, Chow Chows, Pekingese, Bull Mastiffs and English Toy Spaniels.

There has been negative publicity in the media suggesting that their distorted physique means that many suffer from health issues including difficulty breathing needing expensive veterinary care.

We have asked our contributing experts about this and many point out that *all* breeds have some potential health issues that are particular to the breed. Responsible breeding is the key and a number of new health initiatives have been introduced to minimize these possible problems.

In the United States the American Kennel Club (AKC) has a new program called **Bred with H.E.A.R.T.** where breeders commit to:

HEALTH — Certifying that their breeding stock is health tested in accordance with the recommendations of their breed's AKC Breed Parent Club.

EDUCATION — Promising that they will pursue AKC provided or AKC approved continuing breeder education so that they stay current on the best breeding practices, including advances in canine health.

ACCOUNTABILITY — Agreeing to comply with the AKC Care and Conditions Policy, including inspections by the AKC, and promising to share with AKC health testing and continuing education documentation.

RESPONSIBILITY — Accepting responsibility for the health and well-being of the puppies they produce and for complying with all laws regarding the ownership and maintenance of dogs.

TRADITION — Upholding the AKC's tradition of breeding purebred dogs that are happy and healthy.

Members of the Pug Dog Club of America (PDCA) support the Canine Health Information Center (CHIC) registry which is a centralized canine health database sponsored by the Orthopedic Foundation for Animals (OFA). The PDCA recommends the following tests:

1. Hip Dysplasia — OFA Evaluation.
2. Patellar Luxation — OFA Evaluation.
3. OFA or CERF Eye Examination - annually by a boarded ACVO Ophthalmologist.
4. Pug Dog Encephalitis (PDE) — DNA test for Necrotizing Meningoencephalitis.
5. Elbow Dysplasia (Optional) — OFA Evaluation.
6. Pyruvate Kinase Deficiency (PKD) (Optional) — DNA based PKD test results from an approved lab.
7. Serum Bile Acid Test (Optional) — PDCA recommends Bile Acid testing for puppies. Typically a 1-2 hour post-prandial Bile Acid is run at 9-10 weeks of age. If it is elevated, then a repeat test is performed using both fasting and post-prandial samples.

So, what is OFA certification? The Orthopedic Foundation for Animals was established in 1966 by John M. Olin after he found that hip dysplasia was affecting his sporting dogs. The OFA maintains a database for hip dysplasia and now also maintains databases on other genetic disorders as well as performing DNA testing.

Photo Credit: Laura Libner of Lorarlar Pugs.

In the United Kingdom the Pug Breed Council has launched the **Five Star Health Scheme**. The Pug Breed Council was formed in 1995 and is comprised of The Pug Dog Club, The Northern Pug Dog Club, The Wales and West of England Pug Dog Club, The Scottish Pug Dog Club and The West Pennine Dog Club. In 2005 The Pug Breed Council Health Sub Committee was formed and liaises with The Kennel Club on current health issues of the Pug.

"For those interested in the health of their Pug, or thinking of breeding, the Five Star Health Scheme being introduced will be a valued tool in assessing health and suitability for breeding. Moving forward this will help the puppy buyer in selecting a puppy from health-tested parents that have completed the Scheme and attained a certificate. The way in which the Scheme works is as follows:

"The first step is to join the Scheme and register your Pug via the website. You will receive a Visual Health Assessment Form that your Vet completes. Once you have returned this to our Breed Health Coordinator you are able to submit the results of the remaining tests. When all are completed, a certificate will be awarded.

"The five tests are as follows, Visual Health Assessment form (VHA), Patella Score, Pug Dog Encephalitis (PDE), Hemivertebrae X-ray (HV), Brachycephalic Obstructive Airway Syndrome (BOAS).

"For information on the Health Scheme and to enroll your Pug, plus details on buying a puppy you can visit the dedicated website. Julia Ashton (Public Relations Pug Breed Council)."
http://www.pughealth.org.uk

We asked **Gail Saffer of Ragemma Pugs** on what you can do to minimize potential issues: "I have been involved with Pugs since 1984. Always check that parents have been health tested and never buy a puppy unless you can see it with the mother. It's not always possible to see the father, as a breeder might have used an outside dog. I never let my pups go until they are 12 weeks old by which time they would have been fully inoculated, microchipped and preliminary X-rayed to ensure no obvious hemivertebrae—I have now X-rayed eight generations but it can still come out like two people having a normal healthy baby and then suddenly having a spina bifida child, so no guarantees. I always give my new puppy owners a contract information sheet, diet sheet, worming certificate, Kennel Club papers and copies of any health tests that sire and dam have had."

Julianne McCoy of Low Country Pugs: "The Pug is the easiest breed I have ever owned or bred. I am not in a Vets office all the time unless they need a checkup. Eyes are always a problem when they are puppies which makes it very important to keep nails cut short because when playing, Pugs usually aim for the eyes. Breeding has its challenges since they don't always breed naturally and may require a C-Section. Some mothers have to be held down to get them to feed their babies and there are others that are ready to wean them off once the teeth come in."

The Pug Puppy

Bringing a new puppy home is fun, even if the memories you're making include epic, puppy-generated messes! Young dogs are a huge responsibility no matter how much you love them, and they take a lot of work. Pug puppies are possessed with boundless quantities of energy. They play non-stop and they love to chew.

We asked **Annie Sullivan of CASull Pugs** how a Pug puppy would compare to other breeds: "Pugs in general are comical little characters now multiply that by ten when working with a Pug puppy. They should be confined to a crate or a room where there's nothing they can chew and get in trouble with if the new owner can't watch them. They can be stubborn with potty training; I think this is a small dog thing to be honest. I tell my new puppy parents the best way to potty train them is taking them outside every two hours around the clock (yep set your alarm) for two weeks. They are just like having a new born baby in the house!! Pugs are usually food motivated, so after they come in from doing their business (and ONLY if they've actually done their business) give them a small treat. You must be consistent!! Pugs love toys so they need to have a toy box full so they can entertain themselves. But toys aren't all they need ... Pugs were originally bred (and continue) to be companions and they need their people!! Pugs don't mature until they're about two years old so brace yourself. And even then they are smart and always a step ahead of you. I like to give all my Pugs a little bit of peanut butter several times a week because I read peanut butter is good for brain development."

Photo Credit: Rosemary Robles of Pocket Pugs.

Every new pet owner hopes to have a well-mannered, obedient, and happy companion. If there is anything you must understand about your Pug puppy, and this is something I cannot stress strongly enough or often enough, it's this—they can be hard to house-train! This aspect of Pug ownership requires a lot of patience on your part. It may take as long as six months for your dog to "get it," and stop making messes inside.

After that, I would say, **be prepared for the shedding**, it's massive and year round! These dogs are also known to be exceptionally flatulent, so keep the air freshener on hand.

If you don't have the time to spend working with your Pug in the areas that will make him a desirable companion, ask yourself if this is really the time in your life to have a pet. What is your work schedule? Do you have to travel often and for extended periods? Only purchase a Pug if you have time to spend with him.

Initially **you will need to devote several hours a day** to your new puppy. You have to house-train and feed him frequently every day, giving him your attention and starting to slowly introduce the house rules, as well as take care of his general health and welfare. Remember too that treating Pugs like babies is something many owners succumb to and this is not at all good for them.

Certainly for the first few days (ideally two weeks), one of your family should be **around at all times of the day** to help him settle and to start bonding with him. The last thing you should do is buy a puppy and leave him alone in the house after just a day or two. They will feel isolated, bored, and sad, and this leads to behavioral problems.

As well as time, there is a financial cost, not just the initial cost of your puppy. You also have to be prepared to spend money on regular healthcare, potential emergency money in vet bills in the case of illness, as well as equipment such as crates, bedding, and toys.

DID YOU KNOW? Research shows that many dogs have the intelligence and understanding levels similar to a two-year-old child. They can understand around 150 words and **can solve problems**, as well as devise tricks to play on people and other animals!

Heidi Merkli of Bugaboo Reg'd tells us that the most common issues that new owners contact her for, after they have their puppy are: "Diet is the number one issue. Pugs are a toy breed and as a toy breed do require a good quality diet not only to ensure and optimize health, but also to maintain a proper weight. They have little frames and although they think they are a big dog, "multum in parvo," they need a diet that can maintain good nutrition, oral hygiene as well as weight. Diet should never be sacrificed on a Pug it can lead to health issues, so a premium quality dry kibble, cooked diet or raw diet should always be considered!"

Julia Ashton of Zobear Pugs: "Thinking of buying a puppy? Due to the huge love the UK has for this small companion dog, there has been an upsurge in breeders, good bad and ugly. Choosing in haste, a must-have, need-right-now, may bring heartache later on. Stop! Do some research; there are five Breed Clubs in the UK, the Kennel Club Assured Breeders Service, and the Pug Breed Council. Choose a breeder that's a member of one of the breed clubs. We have a Pug Health Scheme so choose a breeder that has health-tested parents. Choose a breeder that is successful in the show ring; the type, the health and overall quality of the puppy will usually be much better than the breeder down the road. Choose a breeder that health tests to the new Five Star Health Scheme, and that provides a puppy pack and contract."

Personality and Temperament

So what defines your Pug's character? One factor is his **temperament**, which is an inherited trait, and another factor is the **environment** in which your Pug grows up. While we can say there are certain traits which are common within the breed, each individual Pug has his or her unique character just like we humans all have a unique personality.

In your Pug's life, the first few months are deemed most important. When the time comes that he is separated from the litter, his reactions and responses to the world around him are a reflection of how he has learned the essence of socialization.

There is no denying the **benefits** that your Pug gets from being introduced early to other dogs and humans along with different noises and smells. When a dog learns how to feel comfortable in whatever type of surrounding he is in, feelings of fear and anxiety can be eliminated. Otherwise these feelings can cause a dog to display undesirable behavior such as aggression.

Pugs pack a massive amount of personality in a very small package. They are not aggressive by nature, but they can be strong-willed to the point of stubbornness. The Pug seems to have the endearing ability to read his owner's mood and act accordingly, either being quiet and calm or vivacious and funny.

Even though a Pug can be a real live wire, the breed has a tendency toward laziness, which accounts for the Pug's often epic struggles with weight gain. Pugs are definitely premier nap and lapdogs, but they will also follow their people around and stay as close to the center of whatever happens to be going on as possible.

Pugs do well with crate training. Getting your dog accustomed to the crate as quickly as possible will cut down on the number of messes you're cleaning up in the first few weeks.

Photo Credit: Christina Hedrick and Cathleen Codling of Wahoo Pugs & Pug Rescue of North Carolina, Inc.

Tannis Postma of Pekeapug Kennels: "Pugs are truly the clowns of the dog world, they love all living things. They bond easily and will love to lay beside you on the couch and allow you to pet them 24/7."

Pugs are gentle dogs that bring joy to elderly people as well as young. In fact many Pugs are used as therapy dogs as **Julianne McCoy from Low Country Pugs** points out: "I bring my Pugs into a nursing home, the seniors will get in their wheelchairs and wait outside their bedroom doors for me to place a Pug in their lap. It brings me so much joy to see that moment of happiness on their faces. Pugs are being trained as service dogs to identify when a child or adult's insulin rises or falls to dangerous levels."

Hilary Linnett of Conquell Pugs: "Pugs are the most loving and jolly breed, always wanting to be part of whatever their family are doing, but able to also be a 'couch potato' and enjoying cuddles and downtime with their family. They are the clowns of the dog world, never a day goes by without them making you laugh at their funny ways. They have little concept that they are indeed a small breed; they have the heart of a lion, and are physically more robust than many other toy breeds of dogs. Their levels of activity often surprise people; they are able to cope with decent length walks if kept fit and not allowed to become obese."

They also have a lot of uniquely Pug "quirks" that first-time owners don't anticipate.

- **Nosy** — Don't be at all surprised if your dog is right under foot wanting to know exactly what you're doing. If a Pug could let loose with a litany of "why" questions like a two-year-old, he would.

- **Food Driven** — Pugs are often so concentrated on finding something edible, they will eat anything, including things they shouldn't, like plastic bottle caps and even rocks. They will quickly swallow such items rather than allowing you to take their "find" away.

- **Paper Addiction** — Many Pug owners report that in proper cat-like fashion, their dogs will shred tissues, toilet paper, and newspapers.

- **Obsessive Licking** — This is a tactile breed that enjoys licking, not just themselves, but anything they can reach including you, your pillow, and even the family cat!

- **Swatting** — Pugs use their paws like hands and will swat at other animals and at you, both in play and as a means to get attention.

- **Endless Commentary** — Pugs have an almost endless repertoire of sounds they use to deliver their opinions on what is going on. This is not confined to barking and howling. They are excellent at pitiful moans, especially when denied food, and trot about grumbling under their breath. (It's very hard to keep a straight face when a Pug grumbles!).

- **Don't Like Bad Weather** — Many Pugs, even after being properly housebroken, will refuse to "go" outside in bad weather. They will either hold it long past what you would think is even possible, or pick a spot on the floor and do their business.

With Other Pets

Pugs get along exceptionally well with other pets, although you may see flashes of jealousy if your very companionable little dog doesn't think he's getting enough of your time. The only real caution I would make in regard to multi-species households is a caution about the Pug's large and prominent eyes. If a cat takes a good swipe at a Pug's face, there is a risk of serious eye damage for the dog, so be extra respectful and careful of Fluffy's displeasure over having a new puppy around until the animals work out some sort of peace agreement.

If anything, the Pug puppy is liable to be guilty of annoying the living daylights out of the cat. Make sure your feline friend has someplace to escape the newcomer before frayed nerves lead to an altercation.

Never force animals to interact or to spend time together. When the Pug puppy first arrives, put the little dog in its crate and allow other pets in the house to check out the new family member on their own terms and at their own speed. Carefully observe the reactions on both sides of the meeting and take your cues from how it's all going.

Supervise all interactions. Reinforce good behavior with treats and praise. At the first sign of aggression or "trash talking," separate the animals with a firm "no" and try again later. Understand this can go on for several weeks until your pets reach some form of agreement whose terms only they will comprehend.

Male or Female?

Typically my position on gender is that **it doesn't matter**. Concentrate instead on the **personality** of the individual dog. This line of thinking seems to hold true for Pugs, with no discernible difference in the temperament of females over males. Pugs are individuals, like people, some are brighter than others, some more stubborn than others, some more idle than others. It is nothing to do with male/female. Both sexes are equally affectionate, love-me-do dogs and are always willing to play, joining in with family life. Regarding trainability, again no real difference and they will learn anything for a reward!

The only time gender is important is if you are intending to breed the dog. Otherwise, focus on the individual Pug's personality. In too many instances, people want female puppies because they assume they will be sweeter and gentler. No valid basis exists for this assumption. The real determining factor in any dog's long-term behavior is the quality of its training in relation to its place in the family. Consistency in addressing bad behaviors before they start is crucial.

Female dogs coddled as puppies display more negative behavior and greater territoriality than males. Consider this factor with a grown Pug, especially in a rescue situation. A Pug's temperament needs to match the household to which it is going. So many owners want female puppies, but in many situations a neutered male is a much better fit.

When it comes to dogs like the Pug, there are few physical distinctions between the sexes. The only difference you are likely to notice between a male and female Pug is that the female might be a little smaller than the male. Perhaps for that reason I might suggest an elderly person may be better with a female, as they are, generally speaking, smaller and less strong than a male and so easier to cope with. A boy could get very heavy on your knee after a while. This could also apply to a family with very young children.

In terms of behavior, sometimes male Pugs mature a little more slowly than females, so you might notice more puppy-like behavior from a male Pug puppy than a female once they reach eight to ten months of age. This might affect training—female Pugs that develop faster than males become mature sooner and will likely respond better to training. Male Pugs that are neutered tend to be less dominant than non-neutered male dogs—they may also be less likely to develop problem behaviors.

In general, you should spay or neuter your dog if you do not plan to breed it (but this is **not recommended** before the age of 12 months). Breeding your Pug is not a decision that you should make lightly, and it is definitely not something you should do if your only reason is to make a profit.

To find subtle differences between the genders, I look to "pack behavior" in the wild. Females will focus on only one male in terms of breeding. Males will focus on all females available for breeding. This can result in females sometimes having a special fondness for one member of the family. Males do not. Having said this, the influence is so slight in a human family one may not notice this, especially if all members of the family give the puppy lots of attention and interaction. I tell families that if they have a situation where one member of the family is gone all week, coming home on weekends only, they may want to consider a male who won't really "notice" this absence during the week.

David and Judith Johnson of Foursquare Pugs: "I personally love the boys. Both sexes are extremely affectionate and loyal, but the girls tend to be more into themselves—true divas—whereas the boys are more into their humans. I have girls that sleep in my bed (for their own comfort), but boys who just want to see me for no reason at all."

With Children

Pugs get along extremely well with children. The dogs don't just tolerate kids. They seem to truly love them. Pugs are sturdy little animals that are up for a lot of play time.

An advantage that the Pug has over many of the other breeds of dog is his medium size and short coat. The Pug is a perfect size to fit on your lap and isn't too big for most children to safely play with.

I always tell families, especially those getting a pet for the first time, that it's extremely important to educate the children on how to treat animals of all types with kindness and respect. Make sure your children understand that the Pug's large eyes can be easily injured.

As is true for any dog, it is important that you supervise any interaction between your children and the dog. A dog of any type only reacts to the stimuli it encounters and filters through its understanding of the world. If a child hurts any dog by pulling its ears or tail or even biting the creature, the dog can hardly be blamed for reacting, but you'll find that a Pug will put up with quite a lot and maintain his perfect humor.

Teach your children how to properly handle a dog, especially when it is still a puppy, to prevent incidents. Don't tolerate rough or aggressive play from either, and explain to children that Pugs like "nice touches." When puppies get too rough or mouth their fingers when teething, respond with a firm, "No!" Soon enough, all parties will get the point.

As good as this breed is with children, my general advice to all potential dog owners is to wait until your children are four to five years of age, when they are old enough to understand the Pug's disposition and to respect his boundaries. Puppies and very small children are hard work!

Children also need to understand any dog needs space at times. Here is where an indoor kennel or crate can be made into a den for the new addition to retire to for some peace and quiet. All children should be taught that every dog sometimes needs time alone.

Even if you do not have children, it is advisable to expose your dog to children during puppyhood to prepare the animal to behave correctly during any future encounters. Being good around children is a critical part of any well-behaved dog's repertoire of manners.

For prospective owners with young children, I'd encourage them to select a puppy from a breeder who has socialized their dogs with children of all ages. This helps to make sure the puppy is confident enough around children to tolerate their odd sounds and movements. Temperament is key—a shy, reserved, or anxious puppy should never be considered for a home with children.

We asked **Julianne McCoy of Low Country Pugs** about the suitability of a Pug in a family with young children: "Pugs are great for young children when the children are introduced to a Pug and not the other way around. The worry is that when you bring a puppy into a home with small children (five to seven), the children can overwhelm the Pug. A small child does not understand not to poke at a Pugs eyes and that they cannot pick up and drop. However, when a child is introduced at birth to a Pug that is already in the home, they adjust very well as the small child grows up and the Pug will oversee the small child. Introducing a Pug to a family with children seven and older is very suitable especially for a puppy but children need to be explained the boundaries.

"I am from the South eastern part of the United States where we can over 100-degree weather, which can be deadly for a Pug. I would never recommend placing a Pug in a family with young children that have never had a Pug, and that are only getting the Pug for the children. Eventually these parents will pass the responsibility of caring for the Pug on to the young children who are not responsible enough to take care of the Pug. Ultimately if something goes wrong, the Pug will lose. I have to make sure that research on the Pug breed has been done and that the responsibility is going to be provided by the entire family. A Pug should never be left unattended outside in over 100-degree weather. Every Pug owner should understand what to do if their Pug gets overheated."

Chapter 2 — The History of the Pug

The Pug breed is believed to have developed in China but the exact origins are unknown as Emperor Qin Shi Huang, the first Emperor of China, destroyed all records, scrolls and art related to the Pug during his reign. According to the London Zoological Society, the Pug is one of the oldest dog breeds in the world. Ancient Chinese documents state that short-nosed dogs with the description matching that of the Pug existed in China at around 600 BC. These dogs would have looked very different to the Pug that we know today.

Originally bred to be a stationary pet and sit on the lap of the Emperor of China, it is believed that the Chinese enjoyed the breed because they could make out Chinese characters in their unique facial wrinkles.

Photo Credit: Children of the Marquis de Béthune with a Pug 1761.

Treasures, like pearls, jade, rare animals or dogs were considered imperial property. One emperor, Ling To (168–190 AD), liked them so much, that he gave these small dogs rank, the females received the same rank as his wives. He ordered that these small dogs were to be guarded by soldiers and fed only the best meat and rice, evidence that

Pugs have always been pampered! If anyone attempted to steal one of these dogs, he or she would be sentenced to death.

Pugs began making their way into Europe during the late 1500s; initially by Dutch merchants, and then by the 1700s, Portuguese, Spanish, and English ships were also carrying Pugs as cargo. The growing popularity of the Pug during the 1700s is due in part to the dog's size, portability, and temperament and its relative scarcity compared to native breeds. Pugs frequently appeared in paintings from this era.

Prince William of Holland (William of Orange) was awakened by his Pug Pompey to warn him of the presence of Spaniards during the war that stretched from 1571 to 1573. By saving his life, Prince William declared the Pug as the official dog of the House of Orange. The breed was called *Mopshond* by the Dutch and is still used to this day. These dogs were often referred to as "Dutch Pugs" or "Dutch Mastiffs."

In 1688, when William III and Mary II left the Netherlands to accept the British throne, a Pug went with them. In time, the dogs became popular throughout Europe.

Josephine, Napoleon Bonaparte's wife, owned a Pug named Fortune and he was responsible for ruining their wedding night. Allegedly, Napoleon requested that Fortune did not sleep in the bed with them, and Josephine stated that if Fortune didn't sleep in the bed, neither would she!

Photo Credit: William Hogarth with his Pug, Trump, in 1745.

The breed's somewhat fanciful appearance led them to be used in interesting ways. In Italy, for instance, Pugs were employed as carriage dogs, dressed in clothing to match the coachman's uniform! While thought of today as a toy companion or "lap" breed, Pugs have done their fair share of work. The dogs have been used by the military as trackers and they were also used as watch dogs.

As the Pug's popularity spread throughout Europe, it became known by different names: In France, the Carlin; in Spain, the Dogullo; and in Italy, Caganlino.

There is a bizarre story of a Masonic society founded by Roman Catholics in Germany known as the *Mops-Orden,* or Order of the Pug, founded in 1740 by Klemens August of Bavaria. The Pug was chosen as a symbol of loyalty, trustworthiness and steadiness. Members called themselves Mops (German for Pug). Novices were initiated wearing a dog collar and had to scratch at the door to get in. They were

blindfolded and led around a carpet with symbols on it nine times while the Pugs of the Order barked loudly to test the steadiness of the newcomers. During the initiation, the novices also had to kiss a Pug's (porcelain) backside under its tail as an expression of total devotion. Members of the Order carried a Pug medallion made of silver. In 1748 the Order was banned.

In the early 1800's, Pugs were standardized as a breed with two lines becoming dominant in England. One line was called the Morrison line and, reportedly, was founded upon the royal dogs of Queen Charlotte, wife of George III. The other line was developed by Lord and Lady Willoughby d'Eresby, and was founded on dogs imported from Russia or Hungary.

Pugs became very popular during the Victorian era and were featured in many paintings, postcards, and figurines of the period. They were often depicted wearing wide, decorative collars or large bows around their short, thick necks. In the UK until 1877, the breed was seen only in fawn but that year a black pair was introduced from the Orient.

Pugs appeared in the artwork of William Hogarth, including his self-portrait dated 1745 that hangs in the Tate Gallery in London.

In the 19th century, Queen Victoria kept many Pugs, even breeding the dogs. Her Majesty's enthusiasm for dogs in general helped to support the establishment of the Kennel Club in 1873, which remains the governing canine body in the United Kingdom today. She preferred the apricot and fawn coloring over the black Pugs.

Many of the Pugs that appear in paintings from the 18th and 19th century had longer legs and faces than the modern breed. Many had their ears clipped, a practice banned in England in 1895. Pugs were also painted by the famous Spanish artist Francisco Goya (1746-1828). The painting of the Marquesa de Pontejas features a well-put-together Pug with cropped ears, wearing his campanula collar (campanula refers to a plant genus bearing bell-shaped flowers). The original painting is on display in the Andrew Mellon Collection at the National Gallery of Arts in Washington, D.C.

Pugs were first exhibited in England in 1861. In China, Pugs continued to be bred by the royal families. When the British overran the Chinese Imperial Palace in 1860, they discovered several Pugs, and brought some of the little dogs back to England with them. Two Pugs named Lamb and Moss were brought to England. These two 'pure' Chinese lines were bred and produced Click. This outstanding Pug was bred many times to dogs of both the Willoughby and Morrison lines. Click is credited with making Pugs a better breed overall and shaping the modern Pug as we know it.

In his book *Dogs of China and Japan in Nature and Art*, published in 1921, V.W.F. Collier has a chapter on "The Chinese Pug", in which he refers to the Pug as the Lo-Sze.

Here is a brief extract: "One of the most important characteristics of the Chinese Lo-sze dog, in addition to universal shortness of coat, is elasticity of skin existing in a far greater degree than with the 'Pekingese.' The point most sought after by Chinese breeders was the 'Prince' mark, formed by three wrinkles on the forehead with a vertical bar in imitation of the Chinese character for Prince (today called the thumbprint). This same character is distinguished by the Chinese in the stripes on the forehead of the tiger, which, in consequence, is the object of superstitious veneration among the ignorant. The button, or white blaze, on the forehead was also encouraged in the Lo-sze dog, but was not of the same importance as the wrinkles."

The Duke and Duchess of Windsor (Edward VIII and Wallis Simpson) were passionate owners of dozens of Pugs in the 1950s and 60s. These really were the ultimate pampered Pugs, drinking from silver dog bowls, sleeping on monogrammed bed linen and wearing silver collars. When the Duke died in May 1972, his remaining Pug named James, reportedly mourned until he eventually died of a broken heart.

The Pug arrived in the United States shortly after the Civil War. The American Kennel Club recognized the breed in 1885, but the breed made a very slow start exemplified by the 1920 number of AKC registrations - just five Pugs!

The Pug Dog Club of America was not founded until 1931 and the 50s and 60s brought about a large increase in popularity.

Member and renowned Pug judge **Patrick Archer McManus:** "Our club has been very active in Pug rescue, health and well-being. We American breeders and our club have gone above and beyond in all regards as well as breeding and showing gorgeous healthy animals that represent our standard and ensure health as well as we can."

You may well come across the name Margery Shriver, who began breeding Pugs in 1961. Sheffield Pug bloodlines can be seen in the top kennels in the USA and other countries around the world and have produced hundreds of champions.

Although a Pug has yet to win at the famous Crufts show in the United Kingdom, in 1981, Ch. Dhandys Favorite Woodchuck, owned by Robert

A. Hauslohner, became the first Pug to win the famous Westminster Kennel Club Show in the USA.

It's uncertain when Pugs arrived in Australia but it was in the mid-1800s, as the first known exhibition of Pugs was in 1870 at the New South Wales Agricultural Show.

Of course the Pug has been in plenty of movies and there is probably none more famous than 'Frank' from the *Men in Black* movies.

Julianne McCoy of Low Country Pugs: "I did some research and found some old books from later 1800s and early 1900s that were in the South Carolina state library. I found out that the fawn Pug came from China and the black Pug came out of Japan. An emperor in China centuries ago gave an emperor in Japan a fawn pug and then several generations later a black Pug appeared. They had a temperament of a terrier and tended to be larger and lot more leg."

"One of my favorite stories is this: One of the most famous Lo-Sze dogs (Pugs) was named Tao Hua or Peach Flower. Emperor T'ai Tsung received Tao Hua as a gift from a Sichuan official from Ho-Chow, which is fifty miles north of Chungking.

Photo Credit: Portrait of Sylvie de la Rue circa 1810.

Peach Flower, regarded by the emperor with the utmost esteem, followed him everywhere. This intelligent little Pug informed everyone of the emperor's arrival by his bark. When Emperor T'ai Tsung passed away, the heartbroken Peach Flower would not accept the new emperor, Chin Tsung. As a sign of mourning, the emperor commanded that an iron cage with soft, white cushions be made for Peach Flower. This cage, containing Peach Flower and the imperial chair, was carried to Emperor T'ai Tsung's tomb. There Peach Flower died. Emperor Chin Tsung, firmly adhering to the doctrine of Confucianism, issued a decree. It was ordered that Peach Flower be wrapped in the cloth of an imperial umbrella and buried beside Emperor T'ai Tsung."

Famous Pugs and Their Owners

Pugs are so popular they've managed to get front and center and in the public spotlight in the company of many famous people and celebrities. A short list of famous Pug owners includes:

- Marie-Antoinette
- William Hogarth
- Queen Victoria
- Harriet Beecher Stowe
- Sir Winston Churchill
- Edward VIII and Wallis Simpson
- Tori Spelling
- Jessica Alba
- Dennis Quaid
- Billy Joel
- Mickey Rourke
- Paula Abdul
- Rob Zombie
- Ted Danson
- Paris Hilton
- Hugh Laurie
- Jenna Elfman
- Kelly Osbourne
- Mackenzie Phillips
- Jonathan Ross

Chapter 3 — Is the Pug the Right Dog?

When you have moved past the stage of just "window shopping" for a dog and think you're pretty well settled on a Pug, there are questions you need to ask yourself, and some basic education you should acquire.

Photo Credit: David and Judith Johnson of Foursquare Pugs.

For people looking for small dogs with low exercise needs that will do well living in a variety of spaces, the Pug is an excellent choice. Although they can act like perfect little imps, the breed also knows when to be calm and even dignified. They are always good natured and amiable, but can become difficult if overly spoiled.

Think of a Pug as a highly intelligent and likable child and raise him accordingly, including knowing when to say no. Overall, you'll have a peaceful companion that only occasionally lets loose with a bark when a visitor arrives. The real welcome will be a symphony of snuffles, snorts, and grunts. Pugs love it when company comes over!

With their large expressive eyes and wrinkled foreheads, Pugs are almost irresistible, especially when they cock their heads to the side and look at you with innocent curiosity. Beware, however, that very tendency makes them expert beggars. Pugs pack on the pounds easily, so avoid letting that business get started.

Although adults will sleep most of the day, your Pug will want to be with you when you're home. They get along fine with other animals, but may be jealous if they think they're not getting enough of your attention.

If you can live through the challenge of housebreaking this breed, and you're prepared for a little dog that can be a real stinker in terms of passing gas, Pugs are excellent and fun companions.

Pug "people" need to be patient, loving, and flexible dog owners who are committed to training their pets and to creating an environment for them that supports their well-being, their best behavior, and gives them emotional security.

You also must understand that you could be signing on for a **10–15-year (or more) relationship** with an intelligent and fairly demanding little dog. Understand from the beginning that your Pug will not settle down and become an adult emotionally for 12–18 months. Many owners give up on their Pugs during this crucial period of life, choosing instead to give the dogs away or to abandon them at shelters.

Think about what's going on in your own life. Don't purchase a dog at a time when you have a huge commitment at work or there's a lot of disruption. Dogs, especially very smart ones like Pugs, **thrive on routine**. You want adequate time to bond with your pet, and to help the little dog understand how his new world runs.

Pugs can be neurotic, aggressive, or fearful (just like any other dog) if they have come from the wrong background and not been nurtured properly. The only way to avoid getting a dog with these issues is to work with a reputable breeder that has a well-developed breeding program. Although dogs from such establishments are typically more expensive, the extra cost is more than worth it in the long run.

Julia Ashton of Zobear Pugs: "Can you offer a puppy/adult the right home? Pugs have been bred for thousands of years as a companion dog, with this in mind if you are out at work all day this breed will not suit you, they need that human companionship all day every day. They require plenty of exercise; the myth of them being fat lazy dogs is untrue. They are greedy and if left unchecked they will pile on the pounds which can affect their breathing causing health problems. They require a good diet and plenty of exercise; they are high energy, busy young dogs. They do slow down when older so maybe an older Pug from a rescue might be right for you. Do you have the time or the family unit to care and occupy the Pugs temperament? A secure garden for the fine weather is a must."

We asked some of our contributing breeders some questions to help you decide if the Pug is the right dog for you.

Is the Pug suitable for a person or family that works all day?

David and Judith Johnson of Foursquare Pugs: "I personally, do not believe any breed of dog is suitable for a family that works all day. Before we sell a puppy to anyone who is not home during the day, we insist that they find a suitable, reputable, dog caretaker/walker or puppy daycare center for the pup they wish to buy. We ask them to send the information on the above with references. If they are unwilling to do that homework, they do not get one of our puppies.

"We also do not sell any puppy before 12 to 16 weeks of age or older. As a veterinarian and vet tech we want our Pugs to have a good start on most of their inoculations before they leave us. With all the "designer" breeding, disposable mentality of some of today's public and the fear of the pups not getting the proper care, selling dogs has become a heartbreaking chore. Sometimes we feel like private investigators with all the questions and references we ask for, but one can never be too cautious when selling a piece of your heart!"

Is the Pug breed suitable for a first-time dog owner?

Doris Klingbeil of Gibby Pugs: "Yes, the Pug is small, easy to maintain, requires very little grooming, enjoys intense activity, but is content to stay at home. The Pug demands a lot of attention but rewards you with plenty of laughter and companionship."

Hilary Linnett of Conquell Pugs: "The Pug is suitable for a first time dog owner, providing they have researched the breed thoroughly and it is suitable for their lifestyle and expectations of a dog. Also, most importantly new owners should only look to buy their Pug from a well-established breeder who carries out all the necessary health tests on their breeding stock, this will go some way to minimise the health risks of known conditions showing in the new puppy."

Does the Pug make for a good guard dog?

Tannis Postma of Pekeapug Kennels: "They will bark if someone comes to the door, not because they want to protect you; they want to see who their next love victim will be."

Can the Pug be described as greedy and prone to weight issues?

Doris Klingbeil of Gibby Pugs: "Of course the Pug is greedy. Most Pugs have a very hearty appetite and are not picky about food. (This in itself contributes to weight gain.)"

Do I Need a License?

Some countries have strict licensing requirements for the keeping of particular animals. Even if you are not legally required to have a license for your Pug, you might still want to consider getting one because it means that there is an official record of your ownership so, should someone find your dog when he gets lost, that person will be able to find your contact information and reconnect you with him.

In the US most dog licensing laws are local ordinances, usually by county, not state. Many municipalities (such as in rural areas) don't require dog licensing at all. Prospective owners should check with their county or city to find out what is required; although if necessary they are usually inexpensive (generally around $25). A rabies vaccine is almost always required by law.

No license is needed to own a dog in the UK, although it is mandatory to microchip all dogs over eight weeks, so any Pug you buy or adopt must already be chipped. It is also a legal requirement in the UK for any dog to wear a collar and tag in a public place.

Puppy or Adult Pug?

After you decide that you want a Pug, you still have an important decision to make—do you want to purchase a puppy or an adult dog? There are pros and cons to each side of the issue, so you should think carefully before you make your decision.

People love puppies for all the obvious reasons. They are adorable, and the younger the dog when you buy him, the longer your time with your pet. At an average lifespan prediction of 10–15 years, Pugs are long-lived in relation to their size.

When you purchase a Pug puppy, you get to raise the puppy in whatever way you like—you have the power to influence his temperament through socialization, and you can also train him as you like. A downside to puppies is that their personalities may change as they grow and develop. Picking a puppy based on personality may backfire because the adult dog could be very different from the puppy.

While raising a Pug puppy can be fun and exciting, it is also very challenging. If you purchase a puppy, you will have to deal with things like teething, potty training, and obedience training. Puppies tend to get into mischief, so you might have to deal with problem behaviors like chewing or whining.

Buying or adopting an adult Pug will not necessarily spare you from all of these challenges, but the dog will probably already be housebroken and might have some training under its belt.

When you do take in a rescue dog, find out as much as possible about the dog's background and the **reason for its surrender**. Pugs are often given up for **behavioral issues**. If these problems are a consequence of environment or treatment, however, it may be possible to correct them.

Not all rescue dogs are 'problem dogs.' Some are wonderful dogs whose owners could no longer care for them for a variety of life circumstances, such as relocation, military service, or going into a nursing home. Occasionally rescues get purebred Pugs with papers, pregnant mothers, or puppies. Expect to go through an application process including home evaluation (where many times the rescue will be looking at such things as adequate fencing). Rescue Pugs typically cost $150–$300, which includes spay/neuter, microchip, and updating all medical care including vaccines. All in all, the rescue will have far more money invested in each Pug on average than the adoption fee covers.

Adopting an adult dog is a good idea because there are millions of homeless pets living in animal shelters, so adopting an adult dog rather than buying a puppy will help to reduce the unwanted pet population. In adopting a Pug you **could also be saving the dog's life**—most shelters do not euthanize pets anymore, but some still do.

A word of warning however—while Pugs are loveable additions to families they are not our children! We disrespect them by not allowing them to fully be the creatures they were intended to be. Dogs need a "job to do" in order to be fulfilled, happy companions. **People create "problem dogs"** that fill shelters by asking them to fulfill human emotional needs! Many dogs are asked to be in alpha positions because humans do not understand the nature of the pack. A family is the "pack" to the dog and the dog needs to understand their JOB in the pack. Truly, the only way dogs achieve the respect they deserve is when we allow them to be the creatures they were created to be.

I don't mean to put you off, but consider some factors please before you make this enormous decision. Just think of how awful it would be for a rescued Pug to be abandoned again because his owners could not cope! This **isn't a way of getting a cheap Pug** and going in with that mentality is so wrong. Even rescue centers may charge an admin fee, but on top of that there are vaccinations, veterinary bills, worming, spaying or neutering to consider. Can you really afford these?

Christina Hedrick and Cathleen Codling of The Pug Rescue of North Carolina, Inc and Wahoo Pugs has some rescue tips and advice: "When looking to add a dog to your family it is important to also consider adopting a rescue. Often-times a puppy is not a good option or fit into your schedule. Whereas a rescue is already used to a schedule and can readily adapt into your home. The rescue organization can help find a dog that will be a great match for you.

"If money is an option then it is cheaper to adopt a dog from a rescue than a breeder. These dogs already come vetted, spayed or neutered, up to date on shots, heartworm negative, so you know what you are getting. If there are any medical needs then you know up front and you are prepared for them. Unlike if you get a puppy from the breeder you have no idea what to expect and you must train them. If you do not have time to train them, oftentimes a rescue will have an adult dog that already has good indoor manners and can walk well on a leash. If you have another dog, then for some it is easier to adopt a dog that has been already socialized with other animals than to try and introduce an unruly new puppy.

"By adopting a dog you are saving a life and this can be the most rewarding thing. You will be forever changing their life in a positive way and it will be just as rewarding for you. So next time you are looking for a new family member consider a rescue. No matter the breed or the age there is a rescue out there needing a home. Adopt a Pug ... Save a Life."

One or Two?

When you're confronted with an adorable litter of Pug puppies, your heart may tell you to go ahead and get two. Listen to your brain! Owning one dog is a serious commitment of time and money, but with two dogs, everything doubles: food, housebreaking, training, vet bills, boarding fees, and time.

The doubling of the housebreaking caution is one you really must take seriously. Most Pugs are not house-trained before six months of age. Are you really up to dealing with two dogs making messes in the house?

Photo Credit: Hilary Linnett of Conquell Pugs.

Jenny Duffy of Kalmadray Pugs: "I would advise that expectant Pug puppy parents opt to bring only one puppy into the family at a time. This increases both the bond to the new owners, and the trainability of the Pug puppy in the long run. They do say that Pugs are like potato chips though and it is perfectly acceptable to add a new addition to the family once the current Pug has established his or her place in the pack so to speak."

The Need for Socialization

Any breed, no matter how well regarded for its temperament, can still develop bad habits and become obnoxious. Pug puppies are fun and energetic, but like youngsters of any sort, they will test the boundaries to see what they can get away with. Pugs will quite happily get away with as much as they can if they get their paws on a compliant human. Your job is to be the "alpha," a responsibility for which many humans are ill-equipped without some in-class time of their own!

Between eight and sixteen weeks is a critical time for puppy socialization. The time and effort you put into this period will pay great rewards during the life of your Pug. I highly recommend puppy kindergarten or some kind of puppy socialization class.

These classes give Pug puppies the opportunity to socialize with other breeds their own age while teaching basic manners. This gives owners a structured approach to working with their puppy and learning techniques to help their puppy become a well-mannered and socialized adult. Contrary to what you may think, dog training is really more about training the people than the dog.

It's important to find a good trainer to help you. Ask your vet and/or call your local kennel club. Try to find a trainer who is a member of the National Association of Dog Obedience Instructors (NADOI) and/or the Association of Pet Dog Trainers (APDT).

http://www.nadoi.org/ or http://www.apdt.com/

Interview the prospective trainer on the phone and ask about their training techniques. You want a trainer that emphasizes positive rewards for good behavior rather than corrections for bad behavior.

Cost of Keeping a Pug

Being a pet owner is never cheap, especially if you stay up to date with vet appointments and feed your Pug a high-quality diet. Before you choose to buy or adopt a Pug, you should make sure that you are able to comfortably cover all of the associated costs.

Upfront costs are the costs you have to cover before you actually bring your Pug home. This includes things like your Pug's crate, his food and water dishes, toys, grooming supplies, and the cost of the dog itself. Ongoing expenses include things like veterinary care, vaccinations, dog license, and food.

You will also need to pay for spay/neuter surgery, and microchipping is recommended (and indeed is compulsory in the UK). Spay/neuter in the UK will cost upwards of £100 at least and is substantially more in the south than the north.

Having your Pug microchipped will cost you about $50, but it is well worth it. Each microchip has a unique number that is connected to a profile that includes your contact information. If your Pug gets lost, whoever finds him can take him to a shelter or vet to get the microchip scanned. Many animal shelters offer microchipping for as little as $15, or microchip them automatically before making them available for adoption.

In addition to the costs already mentioned, you will have to take your Pug in for regular visits to the vet. While he is still a puppy you might have to go every few weeks for vaccinations.

Food is the other important recurring cost. Pugs are small dogs, so they do not eat a lot at one time. While you might be able to find a month's supply of dog food for $15, you shouldn't skimp when it comes to your dog's diet. The quality of your Pug's diet will have a direct impact on his health and wellbeing, so you should choose a high-quality food, even if it costs a little bit more. Giving your dog a healthy diet will cut down on your veterinary costs in the long run because your dog will be healthier.

Pros and Cons of Owning a Pug

Every breed of dog has its own list of advantages and disadvantages. If you are thinking about buying a Pug, you would do well to consider both, although it's a very subjective business since what one person may love in a breed another person will not like at all.

People who love Pugs should be ready to talk about their good qualities, as well as the challenges they pose, for one overriding reason—a desire to see these very special animals go to the best home possible where they will be loved and appreciated. I would rather "put someone off" than see a Pug bought and then slowly neglected over time by a less-than-committed owner.

Pros of Pug Ownership

- Small, sturdy dogs. They don't feel like "little" dogs
- Compact and strong
- Expressive face that conveys personality
- Short coat that is both soft and easy to groom
- Good manners around all types of people

- Excellent with other pets
- Low exercise requirements
- Aren't trouble makers
- Don't get into things
- Adults like to sleep much of the day (but they do often snore)

Cons of Pug Ownership

- Due to their flat faces, these dogs snort, snuffle, wheeze, snore, and slobber
- The breed is "gassy," and can really smell up a room
- They take to housebreaking slowly
- They only shed once a year but it is for 365 days!
- Obesity is a problem
- Challenging to train
- Can be demanding if allowed to become spoiled
- A number of potential health problems

It is imperative that new owners understand the potential for medical problems with this breed. The chapter on health includes a full discussion of such potential conditions.

Belinda Goyarts of Raevon Pugs adds: "Pugs are wonderful but there are issues people never think of, or are misled into believing via websites. These include the inability to cope with heat, very common eye issues, their huge energy level, and the similarity of a Pug and a three year old toddler.

"Bred purely to be a companion dog and weighing up to 12 kilos—they are not lapdogs for indoor loving people who live in a high-rise. They need lots of company, lots of exercise, and access to a fairly healthy bank balance (vet bills) or at the very least—pet insurance."

Tannis Postma of Pekeapug Kennels: "Pugs snore, some worse than others - like our partners in life. To me a Pug snore is as relaxing as a cat purring ... I love it."

Chapter 4 — Buying a Pug

Now that you have decided to proceed with purchasing a Pug, the process may seem daunting and confusing; particularly for people who have never purchased a pedigree dog. How do you select a breeder? How do you know if you're working with a good breeder? How do you pick a puppy? Are you paying a good price?

Photo Credit: Julia Ashton of Zobear Pugs.

These questions are especially important when adopting a popular, small dog like a Pug. The breed has been highly targeted by puppy mills. With their flat, "smooshed" faces, Pugs, like all brachycephalic breeds can have a number of health issues affecting their breathing and the formation of their jaws.

When no thought is given to genetics in pairing breeding animals, the risk for these types of problems is greatly elevated. Pugs are also often available from 'amateur' breeders who, though perhaps well-meaning, may be unknowingly passing on undesirable traits for ill health.

Although the initial expense will be greater, it is definitely to your advantage to work with a high-quality breeder specializing in Pugs. The breed's longevity, often as much as 15 years, is one reason they are highly prized as companions. You want to bring home a healthy puppy, because you're going to fall so completely in love with your Pug, you'll want him with you as long as possible.

Pet Quality vs. Show Quality

First, you need to understand the basic terminology you will encounter to rate puppies that are offered for sale by breeders: pet quality and show quality. Understanding the difference in these designations is often as simple as looking at the offered price. Good breeders do what they do for one reason: a desire to improve the breed.

You will want a breeder to explain to you why the animal is considered pet quality over show quality, but since reputable breeders don't sell unhealthy dogs, this is not a stumbling block, but rather standard procedure. Pet quality puppies are, by their very definition, judged to be inappropriate for use in breeding programs.

The most obvious reason for wanting to buy a show quality puppy is a desire to get involved in the dog fancy and to exhibit your animal in organized competitions. Show quality animals can cost as much as three times more.

It's very important to understand that **you probably won't be able to pick out your puppy** if purchasing from a show breeder. Show breeders breed to have something to show. To that end, they will usually select and keep the most promising show prospect. Other show prospects may be reserved for other show homes. Of the remaining puppies, the experienced breeder will select the best puppy for your home and family based on your needs. For example, the boldest, most playful puppy may be best for a family with active children, whereas a shy or quiet puppy would be better suited to a retired couple.

'Pet quality' puppies are not inferior puppies—they just have minor imperfections that would keep them from being winners in the show ring. A healthy, well-adjusted, loving Pug is a winner in anyone's home; regardless of slight imperfections that the average person would not be concerned about or notice.

How Much Do They Cost?

Prices vary widely. Pug puppies for sale from reputable breeders cost from about $750 to $2500 (£500 to £2000). Most breeders do not list prices on their homepages. Good Pug breeders usually have a waiting list of prospective owners and **do not sell their dogs to anyone**.

Brenda Shellehamer of Brendy Pugs: "A Pug puppy from a reputable breeder in the mid-Atlantic coast of the US will average about $2,000.00 Most reputable breeders do health testing which is why a puppy is much higher than a puppy bought from a newspaper ad or pet store."

We have worked together with many of the best Pug breeders in producing this book. We asked them about their pricing and the consensus was that when looking at the price of a Pug, one must keep

in mind all the costs incurred by a reputable breeder versus a puppy mill. No matter what the initial price, remember this is nothing compared to the long-term ongoing costs of dog ownership.

Photo Credit: Julia Ashton of Zobear Pugs.

Sadly, unscrupulous breeders with almost no knowledge of the breed have sprung up, tempted by the prospect of making easy money. A healthy Pug will be an irreplaceable part of your family for the next decade or more. You shouldn't buy an unseen or imported puppy, or one from a pet shop or newspaper! You may end up saving a small amount in the short term only to find you have a puppy that has health issues that will cost you **thousands** more in the long run.

A **suspiciously low** price means that the Pug is most likely from a "puppy mill" (think factory) where corners are cut, annual specialist exams do not happen, breeders continue to use parent dogs with genetic problems, and puppies are usually crated for the first eight weeks and kept in isolation, meaning no socialization, which could lead to behavioral problems that you get stuck with.

What is important is to ask the breeders about the **testing they do on the parent dogs**, and to ask what the guarantee is against health problems. Get this **in writing before you buy**. You need to base your decision on QUALITY and not price!

The Kennel Club has conducted research with shocking results. Too many people are still going to unscrupulous breeders, with:

• One third of people failing to see the puppy with its mother
• More than half not seeing the breeding environment
• 70% receiving no contract of sale
• 69% not seeing any relevant health certificates for the puppy's parents
• 82% not offered post-sales advice

We strongly suggest you start your search by **looking up your country's national Pug Dog Club**, which are listed at the back of the book under the "useful websites" section.

In the UK, **The Kennel Club Assured Breeder Scheme** promotes good breeding practice and aims to work together with breeders and buyers to force irresponsible breeders, or puppy farmers, out of business. Every single Assured Breeder is inspected by the Kennel Club, a UK AS-accredited certification body, in order to ensure that the Scheme is upheld as the essential quality seal for puppy breeding and buying.

The purchase price of a puppy is just about the last question you should ask a breeder. Yes, we all like to save money, but the time to do it is not when you buy your puppy. You'll almost certainly regret it later.

A responsible breeder put the best genetic material into building your puppy when she chose the sire and dam. They didn't just breed your pup's mother to the dog down the block because he was handy. They studied pedigrees and temperaments and faults and virtues and chose the particular sire that would produce the best puppies when bred to that particular bitch.

Both parents were likely tested for genetic defects specific to Pugs. These problems are not always evident at birth, but can crop up several years later in the most heartbreaking ways. A good breeder cannot absolutely guarantee against all genetic defects, but has chosen as carefully as possible to minimize the possibility of your puppy having them. Before you buy a puppy, you should study the breed carefully and find out what the breed's problems are and whether pre-breeding screening is available.

The mother receives the absolute best prenatal care available, with no expense spared. When the puppies arrive, they are treated the same way. They not only are physically healthy, but are properly socialized and checked for sound temperaments. They receive recommended vaccinations and are checked and treated for worms and other parasites. Show prospects and pets from the litter receive exactly the same care.

When you take your puppy home, it's with a health guarantee and your most valuable resource—instructions to call the breeder with any questions. Having problems housebreaking? Call the breeder. Wonder if a behavior is normal? Call the breeder. Puppy is off his feed? Call the breeder. There is no question so trivial to which a good breeder is not interested in helping you find the answer.

Seldom does a good breeder make a profit on a litter of puppies. What may seem like a large purchase price to you is only a drop in the bucket of expenses the breeder faces in planning a litter. You aren't lining the breeder's pockets when you buy a quality puppy. You are simply helping them continue to afford to breed. Reputable breeders do not breed for the money, but not many of them could afford to breed if they didn't cover at least part of the expenses through pet sales.

How to Choose a Breeder

If you do not have a national Pug organization or club in your country, you will be faced with searching for breeder sites online. Visit breeder websites and speak over the phone to breeders in whose dogs you are interested before you schedule a puppy visit. You want a breeder who is clearly serious about their breeding program and displays this fact with copious information about their dogs, including lots of pictures.

You should evaluate the breeder's knowledge not only of the breeding process but of the Pug breed specifically. Avoid any that seem **unwilling** to answer your questions and those who do not seem to have the best interest of their puppies in mind. Plan on visiting more than one before you make your decision. **Never** buy a Pug that is less than eight weeks old or one that has not been fully weaned.

Finding advertisements for Pugs in local newspapers or similar publications is **dicey at best**. All too often, if you go through the classified ads you can stumble upon a puppy mill where dogs are being raised in deplorable conditions for profit only.

Never buy any dog unless you can meet the parents and siblings and see for yourself the surroundings in which the dog was born and is being raised. If you are faced with having to travel to pick up your dog, it's a huge advantage to see recorded video footage, or to do a live videoconference with the breeder and see the puppies.

It is far preferable to work with a breeder from whom you can verify the health of the parents and discuss the potential for any congenital illnesses. Responsible breeders are **more than willing** to give you all this information and more, and are actively interested in making sure their dogs go to good homes. If you don't get this "vibe" from someone seeking to sell you a dog, something is wrong.

I'm not a great fan of shipping live animals. If possible, try finding a local breeder, or one within reasonable traveling distance. Even if you find a Pug breeder online, visit the breeder at least once before you buy. Plan on picking your Pug up in person from the breeder.

Note that the Animal Care Welfare Act passed in November 2013 gives new laws/guidelines for breeders who ship. They now need to be **federally licensed** by the USDA.

Be suspicious of any breeder unwilling to allow such a visit or one who doesn't want to show you around their operation. You don't want to interact with just one puppy. You **should meet the parent(s)** and the entire litter although note that sometimes you won't be able to see both parents, just the dam (mother). Often the bitch is sent away to an outside stud dog to be bred. Rarely does a breeder breed his own bitch to his own dog. However, you should be able to see photos of the sire and a five-generation pedigree.

It's important to get a sense of how the dogs live, and their level of care. When you talk to the breeder, information should flow in both directions. The breeder should discuss both the positives and negatives associated with the dogs.

Photo Credit: Tannis Postma of Pekeapug Kennels.

Nowadays many breeders are home-based, and their dogs live in the house as pets. Puppies are typically raised in the breeder's home as well. It's also common for breeders to use **guardian homes** for their breeding dogs. The breeder retains ownership during the years the dog is used for breeding, but the dog lives permanently with the guardian family. This arrangement is great for the dog because once retired from breeding he/she is spayed/neutered and returned to its forever family. There is no need to rehome the dog after its breeding career has ended.

What to Expect from a Good Breeder

Responsible breeders help you select a puppy. They place the long-term welfare of the dog front and center. The owner should show interest in your life and ask questions about your schedule, family, and other pets. This is not nosiness. It is an excellent sign that you are working with a professional with a genuine interest in placing their dogs appropriately.

When you go to look at puppies, take your lifestyle into consideration. Pick the puppy that will fit in your household. For example, if you have a quiet household and want a lapdog, or just want to take walks with the dog, pick the puppy with the laid-back personality. They will be content to sit with you more. If you have active children and want a dog to play fetch with them, pick the busy puppy.

You want the breeder to be a resource for you in the future if you need help or guidance in living with your Pug. Be receptive to answering your breeder's queries and open to having an ongoing friendship. It is quite common for breeders to call and check on how their dogs are doing and to make themselves available to answer questions.

I strongly recommend that you take your newly purchased puppy to a vet to have a **thorough check-up within 48 hours**. If there are any issues with the health of the puppy, it will be difficult emotionally, but worth it, to return him to save you from a lifetime of pain, as well as the financial costs in vet bills. Good breeders will have a guarantee for this eventuality in their contract.

Good Breeders Checklist

1. Check that the area where the puppies are kept is clean and that the puppies themselves look clean.

2. They don't breed multiple breeds: two or three maximum. Ideally they only breed and specialize in the Pug.

3. Their Pugs are alert and appear happy and excited to meet you.

4. Puppies are not always available on tap but instead they have a waiting list of interested purchasers.

5. They don't over-breed, because this can be detrimental to the female's health.

6. They ask you lots of questions about you and your home.

7. They feed their Pugs a high quality "premium" dog food or possibly even a raw diet.

8. They freely offer great specific, detailed advice and indicate that they are on hand after the sale to help with any questions.

9. You get to meet the mother when you visit.

10. You are not rushed in and out, but get to spend time with the dogs and are able to revisit for a second time if necessary.

11. They provide a written contract and health guarantees.

12. They have health records for your puppy showing visits to the vet, vaccinations, worming, etc. and certificates to show he is free from genetic defects.

13. They clearly explain what you need to do once you get your puppy home.

14. They agree to take the puppy back if necessary.

15. They are part of official organizations or have accreditations.

16. They have been breeding Pugs for a number of years.

17. They allow you to speak to previous customers.

18. The breeder is willing to provide original official AKC or Kennel Club papers to prove registration.

The Breeder Should Provide the Following

- The *contract of sale* details both parties' responsibilities. It also explains the transfer of paperwork and records.

- The *information packet* offers feeding, training, and exercise advice. It also recommends standard procedures like worming and vaccinations.

- The *description of ancestry* includes the names and types of Pug used in breeding.

- *Health records* detail medical procedures, include vaccination records, and disclose potential genetic issues.

- The breeder should *guarantee the puppy's health* at the time of pick up. You will be required to confirm this fact with a vet within a set period of time.

Seven Warning Signs of a Potential Bad Breeder

1. Breeders who tell you it is not necessary for you to visit their facility in person.

2. Breeders who will allow you to come to their home or facility, but who will not show you where the Pugs actually live.

3. Dogs kept in dirty, overcrowded conditions where the animals seem nervous and apprehensive.

4. Situations in which you are not allowed to meet at least one of the puppy' parents.

5. Sellers who can't produce health information or who say they will provide the records later.

6. No health guarantee and no discussion of what happens if the puppy does fall ill, including a potential refund.

7. Refusal to provide a signed bill of sale or vague promises to forward one later.

Puppy Mills

Such operations **exist for profit only**. They crank out the greatest number of litters possible with an eye toward nothing but the bottom line. The care the dogs receive ranges from deplorable to **non-existent**. Inbreeding is standard, leading to genetic abnormalities, wide-ranging health problems, and short lifespan.

The internet is, unfortunately, a ripe advertising ground for puppy mills, as are pet shops. If you can't afford to buy from a reputable breeder, consider a shelter or rescue dog: you are saving an animal in need.

Be **highly suspicious** of any breeder that assures you they have dogs available at all times. It is normal, and a sign that you are working with a reputable breeder, for your name to be placed on a waiting list. You may also be asked to place a small deposit to guarantee that you can buy a puppy from a coming litter. Should you choose not to take one of the dogs, this money is generally refunded, but find out the terms of such a transaction in advance.

Avoiding Scams

It's so easy to get emotionally charged up about getting a beautiful puppy, and getting really hooked by photos on a website. But, sadly, many people have done just that, and ended up with a puppy that had to be put down because of a serious heart defect, or have extremely expensive surgery to correct patellar luxation, and the seller has offered no refund, full or partial. Parent dogs that are being mated should have been screened for genetic faults prior to being bred.

Photo Credit: Lorna Sale of Poohpugs Perm. Reg.

Many people have paid a lot for a puppy only to discover it has temperament disorders that cannot be corrected, even after spending many thousands of dollars with professional trainers. This is all so avoidable.

People need to know about the health guarantee the breeder offers. What does it cover? All genetic faults? Do you have to return the puppy to the breeder as part of the health guarantee? This is how many breeders get out of honoring their guarantee. They know the buyer will be way too attached to the puppy to return it in order to get the refund.

Always buy from a breeder that has verifiable references from professional trainers or vets. Do a search on the Better Business Bureau website to confirm that the business has no complaints or has settled all complaints.

Verify the breeder's reputation by speaking with other families that have adopted puppies from them to make sure the puppies come from quality adult breeding dogs and that the breeder is honest and ethical. Ask to see the buyer's contract and health warranty documents BEFORE you buy. Go by contract and not just conversation.

Deal directly with your breeder and avoid any middlemen. When considering any business, BE SURE to do a Google search for the business or the website name followed by the words "complaints" or "reviews." If there have been problems, various websites for rip-off reporting and consumer complaints will come up.

Identification Systems for Dogs

Your Pug may or may not have a means of permanent identification on their bodies when they are purchased. Governing organizations use differing systems. The American Kennel Club recommends permanent identification as a "common sense" practice. The preferred options are tattoos or microchips.

Microchipping is perfectly safe and involves implanting a small transponder inside a glass capsule about the size of a grain of rice under the skin between the shoulder blades. When a scanner is passed over the chip a unique number comes up to identify the registered owner (make sure to remember to keep your contact details updated).

Since 2016, microchipping has been made compulsory in the UK for all dogs. All puppies sold **have to be microchipped** by 8 weeks of age, i.e.

prior to purchase by new owners. You must have this done by an authorized implanter. Failure to do so will result in a £500 fine if caught and prosecuted. Costs are not expensive—from trained and licensed microchippers who charge around £15 to vets costing around £25.

Any dogs traveling to or returning to the UK from another country can do so under the Pet Passport system, for which microchipping is a requirement. For more information, see http://www.gov.uk/take-pet-abroad.

What Is the Best Age to Purchase a Puppy?

Pug puppies are born with their eyes and ears closed. Newborn puppies have no teeth and very little fur, so they rely completely on their mother for warmth.

Lorna Sale of Poohpugs Perm. Reg: "The average size of a Pug litter is usually three to five and healthy newborns weigh between 5–6ozs. I had a litter of nine on one occasion with eight surviving. A litter of that size does not normally happen."

A Pug puppy needs time to learn important life skills from the mother dog, including eating solid food and grooming themselves. For this reason, it is harmful to bring puppies to your home too early. These are the key puppy stages.

0–7 Weeks

Puppies typically open their eyes at 14 days, and the ears will also open two weeks after birth. Puppies rely on their mothers not only for warmth during the first few weeks but also for food — they will spend about 90% of their day sleeping and 10% feeding.

Puppies live on a mother's milk-only diet for approximately the first four weeks. He learns discipline and manners from his mother, and littermates help with socialization and learning the social rules of the pack.

A mother will start to self-wean her pups when they are about four weeks old. You can tell when she is ready because she will not want to spend much time in the box with them. As the puppies' teeth emerge, the dam will be more reluctant to nurse. This is normal and helps her milk production to slow down. At this point it is important for the breeder to start supplementing the puppies with a good quality puppy food mixture four times per day. Usually by seven or eight weeks, the puppies are fully weaned from the mother's milk.

Puppies are not able to control their bowels when they are first born, so the mother will lick them to help stimulate urination and defecation.

8–12 Weeks

At about eight weeks the puppies will receive their first vaccine. Because it is not known exactly when the maternal antibodies from the mother's milk will wear off, a series of vaccines is required. Your veterinarian will give you the best recommendations.

The fact is that most puppies go home at eight weeks, but none should ever go sooner than this, as this could result in negative issues such as shyness. A "breeder" doing this may simply want to cash in and turn over lots of puppies too quickly.

From the time the puppies are weaned at about eight weeks, until they are ready for their new homes, their mother and siblings continue to teach them "dog manners." A good breeder will also start basic leash and crate training during the first 8–12 weeks. This helps the puppy adjust to its new home much easier.

Now that the brain is developed, he needs socializing with the outside world, otherwise he can become fearful.

12 Weeks Onwards

Some breeders will insist on keeping the puppies longer (10–12 weeks) to allow the puppy's immune system to become stronger.

During your puppy's change to adolescence, continue exposure to as many different sounds, smells, and people as possible. Begin formal training and obedience, and always praise his good behavior without being too strict or too soft with him.

We asked **Heidi Merkli of Bugaboo Reg'd** when she allows her puppies to be taken home by their owners: "I do not let my puppies go until at least 12 weeks of age, not only to allow the mother and puppy bond to continue, but for other socializations to the environment. It is also important to do further health testing and to grow out the puppies in order to make sure the choices for show/breeding can be carefully considered. All puppies whether show/breeding or companion/pet are evaluated and health-tested during the 12 weeks they are in our care."

How to Choose a Puppy

My best advice is to go with the puppy that is drawn to you. My

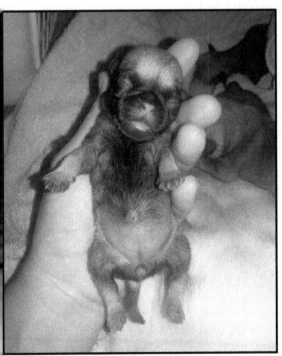

standard strategy in selecting a pup has always been to sit a little apart from a litter and let one of the dogs come to me. My late father was, in his own way, a "dog whisperer." He taught me this trick for picking puppies, and it's never let me down.

Photo Credit: Jenny & Dave Duffy of Kalmadray Pugs.

I've had dogs in my life since childhood and enjoyed a special connection with them all. I will say that often the dog that comes to me isn't the one I might have chosen—but I still consistently rely on this method.

You will want to choose a puppy with a friendly, easy-going temperament, and your breeder should be able to help you with your selection. Also ask the breeder about the temperament and personalities of the puppy's parents and if they have socialized the puppies.

Always be certain to ask if a Pug puppy you are interested in has displayed any signs of aggression or fear, because if this is happening at such an early age, you may experience behavioral troubles as the puppy becomes older.

Beyond this, I suggest that you interact with your dog with a clear understanding that **each one is an individual** with unique traits. It is not so much a matter of learning about all Pugs, but rather of learning about YOUR Pug dog.

Nine Essential Health Tests You Can Use

Before the "Aw factor" kicks in and you are completely swept away by the cuteness of a Pug puppy, familiarize yourself with some basic quick health checks.

1. Although a puppy may be sleepy at first, the dog should wake up quickly and be both alert and energetic.

2. The little dog should feel well fed in your hands, with some fat over the rib area.

3. The coat should be shiny and healthy with no dandruff, bald patches, or greasiness.

4. The puppy should walk and run easily and energetically with no physical difficulty or impairment.

5. The eyes should be bright and clear with no sign of discharge or crustiness.

6. Breathing should be quiet, with no sneezing or coughing and no discharge or crust on the nostrils.

7. Examine the area around the genitals to ensure there is no visible fecal collection or accumulation of pus. If a puppy is dirty from pee or fecal matter then that, for me, is reason to leave quickly without wasting any more of your time, as it indicates poor standards.

8. Test the dog's hearing by clapping your hands when the puppy is looking away from you and judge the puppy's reaction.

9. Test the vision by rolling a ball toward the dog, making sure the puppy appropriately notices and interacts with the object.

Six Great Checks for Puppy Social Skills

When choosing a Pug puppy out of a litter, look for one that is friendly and outgoing, rather than one that is overly aggressive or overly fearful. Puppies who demonstrate good social skills with their littermates are much more likely to develop into easy-going, happy adult dogs that play well with others.

Observe all the puppies together and take notice:

1. Which puppies are comfortable both on top and on the bottom when play fighting and wrestling with their littermates? Which puppies seem to only like being on top?

2. Which puppies try to keep the toys away from the other puppies, and which puppies share?

3. Which puppies seem to like the company of their littermates, and which ones seem to be loners?

4. Puppies that ease up or stop rough play when another puppy yelps or cries are more likely to respond appropriately when they play too roughly as adults.

5. Is the puppy sociable with humans? If they will not come to you, or display fear toward strangers, this could develop into a problem later in their life.

6. Is the puppy relaxed about being handled? If not, they may become difficult with adults and children during daily interactions, grooming, or visits to the veterinarian's office.

Submissive or Dominant?

It is something of a myth that dogs are either submissive or dominant. In reality, they are likely to be somewhere in between the two, but it is helpful to understand where they fit in so you know how to deal with them. Watching how they act around their littermates can give you clues.

Submissive dogs:

• Turn away when other dogs stare
• Are happy to play with their littermates
• Do not try to dominate other dogs
• May show submissive urination when greeting other dogs
• Allow other dogs to win at tug-of-war
• Provide attention and affection to other dogs
• Back off when other dogs want to take food or toys
• Roll on their backs to display their belly

If a Pug shows definite submissive or dominant tendencies, which should you pick? There is no one right answer. You need to choose a puppy that best suits your family's lifestyle.

A submissive Pug will naturally be more passive, less manic, and possibly easier to train. A dominant Pug will usually be more energetic and lively. They could be more stubborn and difficult to train or socialize, but this needn't be a negative and can be overcome with a little persistence.

Dogs are pack animals, and they are happiest when they have structure and they can follow their nature. Followers want to be told what to do and know what the leaders expect of them. Know that you must be the pack leader to your Pug. He should be submissive even to younger children, so aggression and other problem behaviors don't arise.

Chapter 5 — Caring for Your New Pug Puppy

All puppies are forces of nature, and Pugs are no exception. Falling completely in love with your new pet won't be a problem at all. Remaining patient during what can be a six-month housebreaking period could be, however.

Additionally, these are little dogs that love to chew, making puppy proofing your home all the more important. Normal chewing, on appropriate chew toys, is a healthy activity for any dog. Your job is to put a stop to destructive chewing before it becomes a life habit.

This is also the critical period when you must put your foot down and not allow your puppy to become a beggar. Obesity is a serious problem with this breed. Beyond weight gain, however, many human foods are dangerous to dogs.

Bottom line, don't let bad habits get started when a dog is young, or you could be dealing with the issues for as long as 15 years!

Household Poisons

A dog, especially a young one, will eat pretty much anything, often gulping something down with no forethought. Take a complete inventory of the areas to which the dog will have access. Remove all lurking poisonous dangers from cabinets and shelves. Get everything up and out of the dog's reach. Pay special attention to:

- cleaning products
- insecticides
- mothballs
- fertilizers
- antifreeze

If you are not sure about any item, assume it's poisonous and remove it.

Look Through Your Pug's Eyes

Think of a puppy as a bright toddler with four legs. Get yourself in the mindset that you're bringing a baby genius home, and try to think like a puppy. Every nook and cranny invites exploration. Every discovery can then be potentially chewed, swallowed — or both!

Get down on the floor and have a look around from puppy level. Your new furry Einstein will spot anything that catches your attention and many things that don't!

Do not leave any dangling electrical cords, drapery pulls, or even loose scraps of wallpaper. Look for forgotten items that have gotten wedged behind cushions or kicked under the furniture. Don't let anything stay out that could be a choking hazard.

Tie up anything that might create a **"topple" danger**. A coaxial cable may look boring to you, but in the mouth of a determined little dog, it could send a heavy television set crashing down. Cord minders and electrical ties are your friends!

Remove stuffed items and pillows, and cover the legs of prized pieces of furniture against chewing. Take anything out of the room that even looks like it **might** be a toy. Think I'm kidding? Go online and do a Google image search for "dog chewed cell phone" and shudder at what you will see.

Bowel blockages can occur from a Pug eating foreign objects they cannot pass. Some Pugs are chewers. You must be careful about leaving things on the floor or within reach of them. Rope toys, some hard plastic or rubber bones, towels, or any material with string can be deadly to a dog.

If you suspect your pup or dog has eaten something, call your vet immediately, as this could require surgery. Your vet may instruct you to induce vomiting to get it up first. If you see that your dog has no interest in eating, or eats and vomits, it could have a blockage. It may be lethargic, and may also have a tender belly if you rub it. All these are reason for concern.

I stopped using towels as bedding many years ago, as one dog ate part of a towel and could not pass it. The string acts like a saw in the intestines. This can be deadly. I recommend replacing bedding with fleece blankets. They have no string, and if a dog chews it up it will pass the material.

Plant Dangers, Inside and Out

The list of indoor and outdoor plants that are a toxic risk to dogs is long and includes many surprises. You may know that apricot and peach pits are poisonous to canines, but what about spinach and tomato vines? The **American Society for the Prevention of Cruelty to Animals** has created a large reference list of plants for dog owners. Go through the list and remove any plants from your home that might make your puppy sick. Don't just assume that your dog will leave such items alone.

https://www.aspca.org/pet-care/animal-poison-control/toxic-and-non-toxic-plants

What to Name Your Pug?

Have you thought of a name yet? Here are our best breeder tips:

1. Choose something you're not embarrassed to shout out loud in public.

2. The shorter the better. Dogs find names with 1 or 2 syllables easiest to recognize, e.g., Lucky.

3. Long names inevitably end up being shortened so think what they could be now—do you like them?

4. Names starting with s, sh, ch, k, etc. are good because dogs hear high frequency sounds best.

5. Ending with a vowel works well, particularly a short "a" or a long "e" sound.

6. Avoid popular and cliché names.

7. Don't go for a name that sounds similar to a command.

8. If you take ownership of a Pug that already has a name, keep the new one similar sounding for his sake.

Preparing for the Homecoming

Don't give a young Pug full run of the house before it is house-trained. Keep your new pet confined to a designated area behind a baby gate. This protects your home and possessions and keeps the dog safe from hazards like staircases. Depending on the size and configuration, baby gates retail from $25–$100 / £15—£60.

Before you bring your new puppy home, buy an appropriate travel crate and a wire crate for home use. Since the home crate will also be an important tool in housebreaking, the size of the unit is important.

Many pet owners want to get a crate large enough for the puppy to "grow into" in the interest of saving money. When you are housebreaking a dog, you are working with the principle that the animal will not soil its own "den." If you buy a huge crate for a small dog, the puppy is likely to pick a corner as the "bathroom," thus setting back his training.

Crates are rated by the size of the dog in pounds / kilograms. This would be a good suggested size for your Pug:

• 30" x 19" x 22" / 76.20 cm x 48.26 cm x 55.9 cm—40 lbs. / 18.14 kg

Put one or two puppy-safe chew toys in the crate for the ride home along with a recently worn article of clothing. You want the dog to learn your scent. Be sure to fasten the seat belt over the crate. Don't worry Pugs usually love to travel in cars and will get used to it quickly.

In the UK Croft are a good source of crates — they have a range of sizes and types to suit all pockets: http://www.croftonline.co.uk.

Crates are really good things. They are not a prison at all but a safe den for your new Pug to go to when they are tired and would like to rest. They are also good for travelling and visiting friends who may not want your new Pug cruising around the house. I find friends are not so bothered about Pug visits if they are quietly sitting in a crate.

Talk to the breeder to ensure your Pug doesn't eat too close to the journey so there is less chance of car sickness, and when he arrives at your home he will be hungry—always a good start!

It is also a nice touch to get an **old rag or towel** from your breeder that has been with the dam. Leave this with your puppy for the first few days, as her scent will help him to settle in more easily.

Take your puppy out to do its business before putting it in the crate. Expect whining and crying. **Don't give in!** Leave them in the crate! It's far safer for the puppy to ride there than to be on someone's lap. Try if possible to take someone with you to sit next to the crate and comfort the puppy while you drive.

Don't overload the dog's senses with too many people. No matter how excited the kids may be at the prospect of a new puppy, leave the children back at the house. The trip home needs to be calm and quiet.

You may need to make a stop, depending on the length of journey. He will likely be nervous, so cover the bottom of the crate with newspapers or a towel just in case. **Have water** and give him a drink en route.

As soon as you arrive home, take your Pug puppy to a patch of grass outside so he can relieve himself. Immediately **begin encouraging** him to do this. Dogs are pack animals with an innate desire to please their "leader." Positive and consistent praise is an important part of housebreaking.

Although a gregarious breed, Pugs can easily be overwhelmed and nervous in new surroundings. This is especially true of a puppy away from its mother and littermates for the first time. Stick with the usual feeding schedule, and use the same kind of food the dog has been receiving at the breeder's, because their digestive systems cannot cope with a sudden change.

Create a designated "puppy-safe" area in the house and let the puppy explore on its own. Don't isolate the little dog, but don't overwhelm it either. Resist the urge to pick up the puppy every time it cries.

Give the dog soft pieces of worn clothing to further familiarize him with your scent. Leave a radio playing at a low volume for "company."

Photo Credit: Brenda Shellehamer of Brendy Pugs.

At night you may opt to give the baby a well-wrapped warm water bottle, but put the dog in its crate and do not bring it to bed with you. I realize that last bit may sound all but impossible, but if you want a crate-trained dog, you have to **start from day one**. It's much, much harder to get a dog used to sleeping overnight in his crate after any time in the bed with you.

I also suggest you **take some time off work**. For about two weeks this will be your full-time job! Constant supervision is essential to house-train your puppy and to give him company while he gets accustomed to his new home, which can be overwhelming initially.

Remember that your new puppy is essentially a newborn baby — puppies need a lot of sleep! They need their nap time, especially after playing. Also, in the evening keep him up with you so when you are ready to go to bed the pup is as well.

He is also likely to whine for the first few days as he adapts to his new surroundings. Your puppy may well constantly follow you around the house. Just handle him gently, make him comfortable, and give him peace and quiet, allowing him to sleep as much as he needs.

A new puppy may also shiver and not eat. Of course, this is all very stressful for you, but don't panic. Obviously ensure that your Pug is not in a cold place, and put warm blankets in his crate or bed. He will eat eventually.

Try taking the food away if he is not ready to eat, then the next time you put something down, he will be more likely to be hungry.

The Importance of the Crate

The crate plays an important role in your dog's life. Historically crates have been more popular in America than in Europe, however, this attitude is slowly changing. Don't think of its use as "imprisoning" your Pug. The dog sees the crate as a den and will retreat to it for safety and security. Pugs often go to their crates just to enjoy quiet time like we humans do from time to time!

When you accustom your dog to a crate as a puppy, you **get ahead** of issues of separation anxiety and prepare your pet to do well with travel.

The crate also plays an important role in housebreaking. Never ever rush crate training. Don't lose your temper or show frustration. The Pug must go into the crate on its own. Begin by leaving the door open. Tie it in place so it does not slam shut by accident. Give your puppy a treat each time he goes inside. Reinforce his good behavior with praise.

Never use the crate as punishment. Proper use of the crate gives both you and your Pug peace of mind. In time with some patience and training, he will regard the crate **as his special place** in the house.

Some breeders **recommend two crates**, one within earshot or inside the bedroom of a family member, and then the other crate in a medium traffic area on the main floor. You want one that comes with a divider; I block off two-thirds of the crate and only use a third. If you don't do this, the puppy goes to the corner and pees and poops there, totally stopping progress for potty training.

I can also recommend a product called Snuggle Puppy. It is great for calming the puppy in the crate—couple that with a covered crate and the puppy goes right to sleep. Exercise, covered crate and Snuggle Puppy = sound asleep puppy in under two minutes!

From SmartPetLove.com: "Our products incorporate the real-feel pulsing heartbeat technology and warmth to help soothe your pet."

REMEMBER—A little time alone is also good, as Pugs can quickly become used to having constant company. There will always be a family emergency when the Pug can't come and being able to settle quietly on their own for an hour or so is essential.

Our Top Ten Crate Training Tips:

1. Pugs like to be near their family, so initially he will whine and cry simply because he is separated from you and not because he is in "a cage." Any sort of interaction, positive or negative, will be a "reward" to him, so ignore the whining.

2. They appreciate space. Give your Pug enough room to turn around in.

3. Always ensure there is access to fresh water inside the crate.

4. Don't keep them locked up in their crate all day just because you have to go to work—this is unfair.

5. Young puppies shouldn't spend more than 2–3 hours in the crate without a toilet break, as they cannot last that long without relieving themselves. This means you should take them out for toilet breaks during the night.

6. Don't place the crate in a draughty place or in direct sunlight where he could overheat. A constant temperature is best. A

metal wire crate (compared to plastic) is best so air flows through the gaps.

7. Making the crate his bed from day one is best. Put in some bedding so he feels comfortable and warm at night.

8. Initially to crate train him, put some tasty treats in the crate and leave the door open when he dashes in excitedly! Also be sure to feed him his meals in the crate so he associates it with positive emotions. Don't shut the door yet, as that will introduce a negative aspect. Let him roam in and out, and reward him with treats when he goes into the crate.

9. After a few days, you can begin closing the door for short periods while he is eating. Get ready for some possible whining but remember to stay strong! Some treats pushed through the wire as a reward works well.

10. To begin with, just close the door for a minute, no more. In a few days, increase the time gradually so he slowly gets accustomed to the door being closed.

Where Should They Sleep?

I have established that I am firmly behind the use of a crate, but you can also have a bed if you prefer, but most importantly—where will your Pug sleep?

I know some new owners can't resist having them in their beds, but I strongly suggest not giving into this! Yes, they will whine and cry for the first couple of nights, but **this will stop!** Sleeping in your bed could be dangerous: they might wet the bed, and with their relatively short legs **it is potentially dangerous** for them to jump on and off the bed.

I don't recommend it but yes, you could have the crate in the bedroom initially, but why not just start as you mean to go on from day one? Place the crate downstairs I say, and your life will be so much easier once they settle in after a few days.

Go Slow with the Children

If you have children, talk to them before the puppy arrives. Pugs are fantastic with children, but this will be the little dog's first time away from its mother, siblings, and familiar surroundings. The initial transition is important. Supervise all interactions for everyone's safety and comfort.

Help children understand how to handle the puppy and to carry it safely. Limit playtime until everyone gets to know each other. It won't be any time before your Pug and your kids are running around all over the house and yard. You'll be amazed by just how hard it is to actually wear a Pug out!

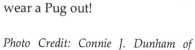

Photo Credit: Connie J. Dunham of MtnAire Pugs.

Introductions to Other Pets

Introductions with other pets, especially with cats, often boil down to matters of territoriality. All dogs, by nature, defend their territory against intruders. This instinct can be just as strong in a small breed as a large one, but with Pugs, the territoriality is often directed toward you.

Pugs are quite capable of being green-eyed, jealous little monsters. They immediately assume the whole place belongs to them and that you are their exclusive property. Existing pets can, understandably, have issues with that attitude.

Neither of these behaviors does anything to facilitate a peace agreement with Fluffy. It's always best in a multi-pet household to let the animals work out the order of dominance in the family "pack" on their own if possible. To begin this process, create a neutral and controlled interaction and first let them sniff at each other from either side of a closed bathroom door.

Since cats are "weaponized" with an array of razor sharp claws, they can quickly put a puppy in his place. A swipe to the nose won't do a puppy any harm, but don't let things get out of hand. Oversee the first "in person" meeting, but try not to overreact.

With other dogs in the house, you may want a more hands-on approach to the first "meet and greet." Always have two people present to control each dog. Make the introduction in a place that the older dog does not regard as "his." Even if the two dogs are going to be living in the same house, let them meet in neutral territory.

Keep your tone and demeanor calm, friendly, and happy. Let the dogs conduct the usual "sniff test," but don't let it go on for too long. Either dog may consider lengthy sniffing to be aggression.

Puppies may not yet understand the behavior of an adult dog and can be absolute little pests. If the puppy does get too "familiar," do not scold the older dog for issuing a warning snarl or growl. A well-socialized older dog won't be displaying aggression with this reaction; he's just putting junior in his place and establishing the pack hierarchy.

Be careful when you bring a new Pug into the house not to neglect the older dog. Be sure to spend time with him away from the puppy to assure your existing pet that your bond with him is strong and intact.

Exercise caution at mealtimes. Feed your pets in separate bowls so there is no perceived competition for food. This is also a good policy to follow when introducing your puppy to the family cat.

What Can I Do to Make My Pug Love Me?

From the moment you bring your Pug dog home, every minute you spend with him is an opportunity to bond. Your Pug has left the warmth and security of his mother and littermates, so initially for a few days he will be confused and even sad. It is important to make the transition from the birth home to your home as easy as possible.

The earlier you start working with your dog, the more quickly that bond will grow and the closer you and your Pug will become. While simply spending time with your Pug will encourage the growth of that bond, there are a few things you can do to purposefully build your bond with your dog. Some of these things include:

1. **Engaging** your Pug in games like fetch and hide-and-seek to encourage interaction.

2. Taking your Pug for **daily walks.** Frequently stop to pet and talk to your dog. Allow him time to sniff and smell during these walks. He is a hound and loves to explore new scents.

3. Interacting with your dog through **daily training sessions**—teach your dog to pay attention when you say his name.

4. Being calm and consistent when training your dog— always use **positive reinforcement** rather than punishment.

5. Pugs love it when you gently **stroke and massage** areas of their body, just avoid the paws, tail and backside. When his body relaxes and eyes close you know you've hit the right spots!

Common Mistakes to Avoid

Don't play the "hand" game, where you slide the puppy across the floor with your hands and they scramble to collect themselves and run back across the floor for another go. This sort of "game" will teach your puppy to disrespect you as their leader—first, because this "game" teaches them that humans are their play toys, and secondly, it teaches them that humans are a source of excitement. A Pug is NOT a toy!

When your Pug puppy is teething, they will naturally want to chew on everything within reach, and this will include you. As cute as you might think it is when they are young puppies, this is not an acceptable behavior, and you need to gently, but firmly, discourage the habit, just like a mother dog does to her puppies when they need to be weaned.

Always **praise your puppy** when they stop inappropriate behavior, as this starts to teach them to understand rules and boundaries. Often we humans are quick to discipline a puppy or dog for inappropriate behavior, but we forget to praise them for their good behavior.

Don't treat your Pug like a small, furry human. When people **try to turn dogs into people**, this can cause them much stress and confusion that could lead to behavioral problems.

A well-behaved Pug **thrives on rules and boundaries**, and when they understand that there is no question you are their leader and they are your follower, they will live a contented, happy, and stress-free life.

Dogs are a species with different rules from us; for example, they do not naturally cuddle, and they need to learn to be stroked and cuddled by humans. Be careful when approaching a dog for the first time and being overly expressive with your hands. The safest areas to touch are the back and chest — avoid patting on the head and touching the ears.

Many people will wrongly assume that a yawning dog is tired—instead the dog is signaling that he or she is not a threat.

Be careful when **staring at dogs** because this is one of the ways in which they threaten each other. This body language can make them feel distinctly uneasy.

Habituation and Socialization

Habituation is when you continuously provide exposure to the same stimuli over a period of time. This will help your Pug to relax in his environment and will teach him how to behave around unfamiliar people, noises, other pets, and different surroundings. Expose your Pug puppy continuously to new sounds and new environments.

When you allow for your Pug to face life's positive experiences through socialization and habituation, you're helping your Pug to build a library of valuable information that he can use when he's faced with a difficult situation. If he's had plenty of wonderful and positive early experiences, the more likely he'll be able to bounce back from any surprising or scary experiences.

When your Pug puppy arrives at his new home for the first time, he'll start bonding with his human family immediately. This will be his **primary** bond. His **secondary** bond will be with everyone outside your home. A dog should never be secluded inside his home. Be sure to find the right balance, where you're not exposing your Pug puppy to too much external stimuli.

If he starts becoming fearful, speak to your veterinarian. The puppyhood journey can be tiresome yet very rewarding. Primary socialization starts between three and five weeks of age, when a pup's experiences take place within his litter. This will have a huge impact on all his future emotional behavior.

Socialization from six to twelve weeks allows for puppies to bond with other species outside of their littermates and parents. It's at this stage that most pet parents will bring home a puppy and where he'll soon become comfortable with humans, other pets, and children.

By the time a puppy is around twelve to fourteen weeks, he becomes more difficult to introduce to new environments and new people and starts showing suspicion and distress. Nonetheless, if you've recently bought a Pug puppy or are bringing one home and he's beyond this ideal age, don't neglect to continue the socialization process. Puppies need to be exposed to as many new situations, environments, people, and other animals as possible, and **it is never too late to start**.

During puppyhood, you can easily teach your puppy to politely greet a new person, yet by the time a puppy has reached social maturity, the same puppy, if not properly socialized, may start lunging forward and acting aggressively, with the final outcome of lunging and nipping.

Never accidentally reward your Pug puppy for displaying fear or growling at another dog or animal by picking them up. Picking up a Pug puppy or dog at this time, when they are displaying unbalanced energy, actually turns out **to be a reward for them**, and you will be teaching them to continue with this type of behavior.

If they are doing something you do not want them to continue, your puppy needs to be gently corrected by you with firm and calm energy, so that they learn not to react with fear or aggression. When the mum of the litter tells her puppies off, she will use a deep noise with strong eye contact, until the puppy quickly realizes it's doing something naughty.

The same is true of situations where a young puppy may feel the need to protect themselves from a bigger or older dog that may come charging in for a sniff. It is the guardian's responsibility to protect the puppy so that they do not think they must react with fear or aggression in order to protect themselves.

Once your Pug puppy has received all his vaccinations, you can take

him out to public dog parks and various other locations where many dogs are found. Before allowing him to interact with other dogs or puppies, take him for a disciplined walk on leash so that he will be a little tired and less likely to immediately engage with all other dogs.

Photo Credit: Vallarie Smith Cuttie of Peachtree Pugs.

Keep your puppy on leash and close beside you, because most puppies are usually a bundle of out-of-control energy, and **you need to protect them** while teaching them how far they can go before getting themselves into trouble with adult dogs who may not appreciate excited puppy playfulness.

If your Pug puppy shows any signs of aggression or domination toward another dog, **immediately step in** and calmly discipline him. Look out for warning signs that indicate a buildup of aggression, which could escalate between dogs: biting of lip, backing away, crouching, growling, fearful posture, tail tucking, snapping, and lunging.

Stopping a Fight

Most owners will instinctually scream loudly at the dogs, but this rarely has an effect and can even cause it to get more out of hand! Stepping into the middle of two fighting dogs can be extremely dangerous and could easily result in physical harm. Here are some tips:

1. Most fights will appear worse than they really are even if there is a lot of noise and motion going on. If there is biting it is usually a quick "bite and then release."

2. Avoid grabbing the head or neck area of either dog with your hands.

3. Place your foot on the rib cage of one of them, push him away.

4. Pull them apart by grabbing their rear ends.

5. Distract them by spraying the dogs with water.

6. Get some object such as an item of your clothing (e.g., your coat) between them or over them.

7. Be careful that the dog or dogs don't turn their aggression onto you!

Take your Pug puppy everywhere with you and introduce them to different people of all ages, sizes, and ethnicities. Most people will come to you and want to interact with your puppy. If they ask if they can hold your puppy, let them, as long as they are gentle. This is a good way to socialize your Pug and show them that humans are friendly.

As important as socialization is, it is also important that your Pug be

left alone for short periods when young so that they can cope with some periods of isolation. If an owner goes out and they have never experienced this, they can destroy things or make a mess because of panic. They are thinking they are vulnerable and can be attacked by something or someone coming into the house.

Safety First

Never think that your Pug would not bolt and run away. Even well-adjusted, happy puppies and adult dogs can run away, usually in extreme conditions such as during fireworks, thunder, or when scared. If he gets lost, it is important he can be identified:

1. Get him a collar with an ID tag because some people may presume that dogs without collars have been abandoned. Note that hanging tags can get caught on things.

2. Put your phone number but not his name on the tag in case he is stolen. A thief will then not be able to use his name. Consider saying, "for reward, call."

3. Inserting a microchip below the skin via injection is recommended, as this cannot be removed easily by a thief.

4. Place recent photos of your Pug in your wallet or purse.

Train your Pug and work with a professional, positive trainer to ensure that your dog does not run out the front door or out the backyard gate. Teach your Pug basic, simple commands such as "come" and "stay."

Create a special, fun digging area just for him; hide his bones and toys, and let your Pug know that it's okay to dig in that area. After all, dogs need to play!

Introduce your new, furry companion to all your neighbors, so everyone will know that he belongs to you.

Know that your Pug will not instinctively be fearful of cars, so be very careful around roads.

Chapter 6 — Pug House-training

This section covers the all-important training of your Pug to go relieve himself outside. This is called housebreaking or house-training, and in America it is often referred to as **potty training**.

When the Pug is born, the puppies relieve themselves inside their den, with the mother cleaning them up so there is never a scent of urine or feces where the puppies eat, sleep, and live. As they get older, they follow their mother's lead in learning to go outside, so house-training may already be established by your breeder when you take your puppy home. If not, they are probably well on the way already. They just need some extra guidance from you.

Photo Credit: Belinda Goyarts of Raevon Pugs.

New owners always ask me how long it will take — there is no timetable for a dog to be totally house-trained. Each pup is an individual and some pick up faster than others. Patience, being consistent in taking them out, and praise when they go are the keys to success. Also, take note on the times the pup needs to go out. This is helpful with taking him out to his schedule.

We have already stressed the importance of being at home for the first two weeks (at least) when you bring your pup back from the breeder. If he is left on his own, expect him to eliminate inside the house because at this stage he doesn't realize that the whole house is not, in effect, his den and not the place to eliminate.

Crate training and housebreaking go hand in hand. Pugs, like all dogs, come to **see their crate as their den**. They will hold their need to urinate or defecate while they are inside.

Establishing and maintaining a daily routine also helps your dog in this respect. Feed your Pug at the same time each day, taking him out afterwards. The feeding schedule dictates the frequency of "relief" breaks. Trips out will also decrease as the dog ages. Don't be rigid in holding your puppy to this standard. Puppies have less control over their bladder and bowel movements than adult Pugs. They need to go out more often, especially after they've been active or have become excited.

On average, adult dogs go **out three to four times a day**: when they wake up, within an hour of eating, and right before bedtime. With puppies, don't wait more than 15 minutes after a meal.

If you are keeping your Pug puppy in a crate overnight, he will need to be let out once or twice a night, as he will not be able to hold it in the whole night until he is aged about four or five months old.

Getting your Pug puppy to go outside from day one is best. Your Pug will want to keep eliminating in the same spot because the scent acts as **a signal "to go"** in his mind. In time this spot will become safe and familiar. Don't allow him to go on your lawn; being soft, he likes this because it feels good under his paws. A discreet corner farthest away from your back door is best, perhaps an area of gravel or, if you live in an apartment, you can use a dog litter tray.

Praise your Pug with the same phrases to encourage and reinforce good elimination habits. NEVER punish him for having an accident. There is no association in his mind with the punishment and the incident. He'll have an uncomfortable awareness that he's done *something* to make you unhappy, but **he won't know what**.

Getting upset or scolding a puppy for having an accident inside the home is the wrong approach, because this will result in teaching your puppy to be afraid of you and to only relieve himself in secret places or when you're not watching.

If you catch your Pug puppy making a mistake, calmly say "no," and take him outside, or to their indoor bathroom area. Resist the temptation to scoop him up, because he needs to learn to walk to the door himself when he needs to go outside.

Clean up the accident using an enzymatic cleaner to eradicate the odor and return to the dog's normal routine. Nature's Miracle Stain and Odor Removal is an excellent product and affordable at $5 / £2.97 per 32-ounce / 0.9-liter bottle.

BREEDER TIP: Try Simple Solutions Stain + Odor Remover, an enzyme cleaner for about £19 / $26 for 4 liters (128 fl. oz.), £5 / $7 for 1 liter (32 fl. oz.)

I'm not a big fan of puppy pads because I find puppies like the softness of the pads, which can encourage them to eliminate on other soft areas—such as your carpets!

Check in with yourself and make sure your energy remains consistently calm and patient, and that you exercise plenty of compassion and understanding while you help your new puppy learn the bathroom rules. Don't clean up after your puppy with them watching, as this makes the puppy believe you are there to clean up after them, making you lower in the dog pack order.

While your Pug is still growing, on average, he can hold it approximately one hour for every month of his age. This means that if your three-month-old puppy has been happily snoozing for two to three hours, as soon as he wakes up, he will need to go outside.

Some of the first indications or signs that your puppy needs to be taken outside to relieve himself will be when you see him:

• Sniffing around
• Circling
• Looking for the door
• Whining, crying, or barking
• Acting agitated

During the early stages of potty training, adding treats as an extra incentive can be a good way to reinforce how happy you are that your puppy is learning to relieve themselves in the right place. Slowly, treats can be removed and replaced with your happy praise, or you can give your puppy a treat when they are back inside.

Next, now that you have a new puppy in your life, you will want to be flexible with respect to adapting your schedule to meet his internal clock to quickly teach your Pug puppy their new bathroom routine. This means not leaving your puppy alone for endless hours at a time, because firstly, they are pack animals that need companionship and your direction at all times; plus long periods alone will result in the disruption of the potty training schedule you have worked so hard to establish.

If you have no choice but to leave your puppy alone for many hours, make sure that you place him in a paper-lined room or pen where he can relieve himself without destroying your newly installed hardwood floor or favorite carpet. Remember, your Pug is a growing puppy with a bladder and bowels that he does not yet have complete control over.

Photo Credit: Steve and Debbie Baldwin of Enchanted Pugs.

Steve and Debbie Baldwin of Enchanted Pugs: "At one time I thought how hard Pugs are to potty train but I no longer feel that way. They are much smarter than we give them credit for. The past few years I've been litter-box training all our puppies, as soon as they can stand, which is about three-and-a-half weeks. I start with a cookie sheet and litter of choice, I use pine pellets and as they grow I give them a bigger box. So, when they wake up, before and again after they eat, and when I see the potty stance, I sit them in the litterbox, for the first few days, while I'm training them, and I watch them closely. It amazes me how quickly they pick it up; usually less than a week they are crawling to the litterbox to go potty. I find the most important thing is to start really young and before they start eating solids, so they don't view the litter as food. Even though some will pick up the litter and put it in their mouth and play with it, I've not had a problem with them actually eating it. A lot of them like laying in the litterbox, but eventually they stop."

Pam Donaldson of Highland/Kendoric Pugs: "Many breeders train their puppies to use a litter box that has paper dog litter or sawdust or pellets. I use paper dog litter and begin litter box training at 3 weeks of age to a boot tray with paper litter kept inside the whelping box. I put them in the litter tray when the puppies first start moving after waking from a nap. They catch on very quickly and this training is not only great for maintaining the cleanliness of the puppy premises, but my adults will use a litter box as well if they can't get outside at the precise time needed. I provide bigger litter boxes for the puppies as they grow up to a full sized kitty litter box. Training a puppy to transition from the litter box to going outside is no different from a transition to outdoors with paper training, i.e. positioning the litter box close to the door. I much prefer litter box training than training to disposable puppy pads which are often joyously shredded shortly after being placed on the floor. Washable cloth pads are cost effective, but I find that if you train the puppies to go on cloth pads, it encourages them to piddle and then mark on clothing, towels, or blankets that might be on the floor. My Pug families who live in apartments, in downtown high-rises, and those who travel frequently appreciate a litter box trained Pug puppy or adult.

"We often have Pugs turned into our Pug rescue with surrendering owners complaining of on-going housebreaking problems. Pugs are no different from most toy breeds which are notoriously difficult to housebreak, so know this before purchasing a puppy. I have found that spaying or neutering often doesn't make a difference when it comes to correcting housebreaking problems. Many rescue Pugs were neutered early, but they still have housebreaking concerns. Both male and female Pugs mark, some more than others and marking with stool is also frequent. Consistency, patience, and a willingness to adapt to them if need be, works. My male Pugs always wear bellybands when they are in the house. I know that the urge to mark is irresistible for the boys because I have intact breeding females in the house. None of my Pugs have the run of the house when I am not able to watch them, because if I do, know I will be shampooing one of my oriental rugs."

Michele Bearden of Charmin Pugs: "We start our litters on newspaper pellets in a very large cat litter box at 3 to 4 weeks of age, then they start outside after their second set of vaccines. That is usually by 10 weeks. The litter training really makes house training much easier and only takes a month or so to get them used to grass! The bladder can't hold urine for more than 4 hours until a Pug gets older. Pugs are very willing to learn, but like any breed being consistent is most important. After they eat, take outside and reward with a treat. Also when they awake take out. Crate training for short periods of time also is a good tool. So patience is the key!"

Bell Training

A very easy way to introduce your new Pug puppy to house-training is to begin by teaching them how to ring a bell whenever they need to go outside. A further benefit of training your puppy to ring a bell is that you will not have to listen to your puppy or dog whining, barking, or howling to be let out, and your door will not become scratched up from their nails.

Attach several bells to a piece of ribbon or string and hang it from a door handle, or tape it to a doorsill near the door where you will be taking your puppy out when he needs to relieve himself. The string will need to be long enough so that your puppy can easily reach the bell with their nose or a paw.

Next, each time you take your puppy out to relieve himself, say the word "out," and use their paw or their nose to ring the bell. Praise them for this "trick" and immediately take them outside. This type of alert system is an easy way to eliminate accidents in the home.

Kennel Training

When you train your Pug puppy to accept sleeping in their own kennel at nighttime, this will also help to accelerate its potty training. Because no puppy or dog wants to relieve themselves where they sleep, they will hold their bladder and bowels as long as they possibly can.

Presenting them with familiar scents by taking them to the same spot in the yard or the same street corner will help to remind and encourage them that they are outside to relieve themselves.

Use a voice cue to remind your puppy why he is outside, such as "go pee," and always praise them each time he relieves himself in the right place, so that he quickly understands what you expect of him.

Exercise Pen Training

The exercise pen is a transition from kennel-only training and will be helpful for those times when you may have to leave your Pug puppy for more hours than they can reasonably be expected to hold it, although we repeat that many of our breeders don't think any dog should be left for more than four hours at a stretch.

Exercise pens are usually constructed of wire sections that you can put together in whatever shape you desire, and the pen needs to be large enough to hold your puppy's kennel in one half of the pen, while the other half will be lined with newspapers, pee pads, or a potty pan with pellets.

Place your Pug puppy's food and water dishes next to the kennel and leave the kennel door open (or take it off), so he can wander in and out whenever he wishes to eat or drink or go to the papers, pan, or pee pads if he needs to relieve himself.

Because he is already used to sleeping inside his kennel, he will not want to relieve himself inside the area where he sleeps. Therefore, your puppy will naturally go to the other half of the pen to relieve himself.

Accelerated Potty Training

This is my advanced, highly detailed guide to house-training your Pug. This is what I recommend for the first four weeks of potty training; after that this needs to be continued but the owner can now give them more freedom.

What I describe below has to be interspersed with exercise and some intensive playtime—at least every few hours. If puppies do not get this freedom to expend their puppy/high energy, at the end of the day, they will be prone to aggressive behavior, including biting and nipping to

try and get their energy out! This develops into a dangerous pattern. As a matter of fact, during training I wake up the puppies and do not let them nap longer than 45 minutes at a time—this will help the puppy expend that pent-up energy all day long.

1. Upon waking up, about 5:30 a.m., even before humans use the bathroom, take your puppy out of the closed crate, scoop him up quickly and take a leash with you. Once he hears you walking about, he will have to "go." Go to a designated outdoor spot and use the same spot for the next few weeks. Put the leash on (I use a leash with a loop at the end because at this age, the puppy's skin gets irritated with a regular collar and he would be very distracted by this.) When you come back in, set the alarm for an hourly schedule. Everything is from the perspective of planning for this hour.

2. Day one will be different than all other days. Please do not use any command when you get outside. Instead, put the puppy down on the ground and wait. He will eliminate. As he is eliminating say the command: "go potty" (this is what I use; it should be a short command).

3. Continue this method all day for the first day. If you do not do it this way, your puppy will have no idea what any command means. You have to say the command while you "catch him" eliminating. Do this many times. Immediately "mark" the behavior with a praise phrase and give a sliver of a treat simultaneously. No treats in the house, just for

potty training. Exceptions are chew treats, veggies, fruits, nothing with caloric content.

4. Day two, you can start giving the command prior to his eliminating.

5. So after the wake-up trip outside, if your puppy does nothing, back in the crate for ten minutes (door closed), then outside again. Keep repeating this every ten minutes until he goes.

6. If your puppy has both urine and bowel movement, and after the treat reward and praise—which must be instantaneous—bring him in. He is again rewarded with complete freedom for ten minutes. After this, he is further rewarded with "limited freedom" for another ten to fifteen minutes inside the exercise pen. If your puppy only does one—either urine or bowel movement but not both, bring him in and he goes straight to the exercise pen only for ten minutes. He does not get complete freedom; he gets limited freedom. During these freedom and limited freedom times, you will want to, several times a day, get into the pen and play very actively with him, and interact with toys as well.

7. After this "reward" time, puppy goes back into the crate, with the door shut. He stays in the crate until that specific hour is up, unless it is breakfast, lunch, or dinner time. Then you start the whole process again.

8. For purposes of potty training, instead of putting him back in the crate for the whole hour, you can hold your puppy as long as you want. You can also let him play outside during this time. Puppies will not eliminate while being held; puppies will eliminate while playing outside but that is ok. This will help you to help him stay awake and expend more of that puppy energy.

9. If it is the first "take out" trip for the day, after your pup has eliminated and while still in the pen, feed him breakfast. Give him ten minutes to eat, and then remove his food. Put him back in the crate after he takes his last bite, have him stay in the crate and after ten minutes, start the potty routine again. After your puppy eats is one of those times that you must take him out again because digestion has

started and moves along quickly; he will have to go again about 10 minutes after eating.

10. So the times that you start the "go potty" trip outside are:

- First thing in the morning
- Ten minutes after each meal
- Immediately upon waking up from a nap (and we do not let them sleep for very long periods, otherwise you will have a puppy who has been crated too many hours during the day and will have anxiety issues at the end of the day)
- Last thing at the end of the day, as late as possible: 10:00 or 11:00 p.m.
- For the first two weeks, every four hours at night or if the puppy cries in the crate
- Keep the hourly schedule for the most part

11. At the four-week mark, you can start expanding the freedom and limited freedom times. You will learn what is best for your puppy.

This method has some "secret" tips that are critical. For example, on day one, it's best not to give any command outside to potty. The pup will have no idea what the person is talking about. Bring puppy out first thing in the morning and just WAIT. Once the puppy starts a bowel movement or starts to urinate, say the command, whatever it is.

Do this for all of day one. If you don't, he won't make the connection very quickly, it will be much slower; I truly believe my pups are 85% on the way after two weeks. Even on the third day, they have made the connection between the command and what we want from it.

Families who follow this training schedule report zero accidents or very few, which they always attribute to their own mistakes. This method works, and if you can put in the initial time, you won't have to worry about struggling with potty training for months and months.

I also find that our Pugs never cry in the middle of the night unless they truly have to pee or poop. And this is usually limited to the first two weeks; when they whine at 2 a.m. you can be sure it is because they have to go potty. Puppies who cry in the middle of the night for other reasons may not yet be confident about the whole training system. The first two weeks we make a point of taking them out about 2 a.m.; then after that, there will be no need. Occasionally they will whine in the middle of the night and definitely have to go depending upon whether their bladder and intestines were emptied out by 10 p.m. or not and how late they ate or drank.

Marking Territory

Both male and female dogs with intact reproductive systems mark territory by urinating. This is most often an outdoor behavior, but can happen inside if the dog is upset. Again, use an enzymatic cleaner to remove the odor and minimize the attractiveness of the location to the dog. Territory marking is especially prevalent in intact males. The obvious long-term solution is to have the dog neutered.

Marking territory is not a consequence of poor house-training. The behavior can be seen in dogs that would otherwise never "go" in the house. It stems from completely different urges and reactions.

Dealing with Separation Anxiety

Separation anxiety manifests in a variety of ways, ranging from vocalizations to nervous chewing. Dogs that are otherwise well-trained may urinate or defecate in the house. These behaviors begin when your dog recognizes **signs that you are leaving**. Triggers include picking up a set of car keys or putting on a coat. The dog may start to follow you around the house trying to get your attention, jumping up on you or otherwise trying to touch you.

It is imperative that you understand when you take on a Pug that **they are companion dogs**. They must have time to connect and be with their humans. You are the center of your dog's world. The behavior that a dog exhibits when it has separation anxiety is not a case of the animal being "bad." The poor thing experiences real distress and loneliness.

Being with him most of the time can cause him to be over-reliant on you, and then he will get stressed when left alone. As discussed earlier, it is wise to leave him on his own for a few minutes every day so he understands this is normal. You can increase this time gradually.

Remember that to a new puppy, you have now **taken the place of his mother and littermates.** He is completely reliant on you, so it is natural for him to follow you everywhere initially.

As well as puppies, you may also see separation anxiety in rescued dogs and senior (older) dogs.

Photo Credit: Wendy Davenschot of Viking Mops, Pugtography.

13 Tips for Leaving Your Pug During the Daytime

Your Pug loves to be with you and he is very much in tune to recognizing those situations where you are going to leave him. He will go through a myriad of antics to avoid being left alone. Being realistic, most of us have to go to work. While we recommend you take a couple of weeks off when you get your new puppy, the time will come to go back to work during the day.

1. Get a neighbor or friend to come in around lunchtime to spend some time with your Pug.

2. Employ a dog walker or come home yourself during your lunch break and take him for a walk.

3. Is there anyone, family, friends, etc. you could leave him with?

4. Exercise generates serotonin in the brain and has a calming effect. Walk him before going to work and he will be less anxious and more ready for a good nap.

5. Leave some toys lying around for playtime to prevent boredom and destructive behaviors such as chewing and barking. Many toys can be filled with tasty treats that should do the trick!

6. Make sure that the temperature is moderate. You don't want your dog getting too cold or too hot in the place where you leave him.

7. Don't leave food down all day—he may become a fussy eater. Set specific meal times and remove it after 15–20 minutes if uneaten. This doesn't apply to water—make sure he has access to water at all times.

8. Leave him where he feels most comfortable. Near his crate with the door open is a good option.

9. Play some soothing music on repeat. There are dog-specific audio tracks that claim to ease separation anxiety. Often a dog will become concerned in a totally quiet environment and that may amplify their anxiety.

10. Stick to the same routine each day. Don't overly fuss him before you leave OR when you return. Keep it low-key and normal.

11. Do your leaving routine such as putting shoes on, getting car keys, etc. and go out and come back almost immediately to build this experience into their brain gradually. Steadily increase the length over time. Do this almost as soon as your puppy comes home, so it won't be such a shock to him when you really do need to leave him alone.

12. Make sure other family members do things with your Pug, e.g., feeding, walking, playing, so he doesn't become over reliant on you.

13. Never punish him. They may do some bad things, but this is not their fault and they do not mean to be bad on purpose. You WILL make the situation even worse if you do this.

Chapter 7 — Food and Exercise

This is perhaps the most important chapter in the book because whatever you feed your Pug **affects the length and quality of his life.** Remember too that they are driven by food so will eat pretty much anything put in front of him; and he will eat as much as he can, so it is down to you as to what type of food he eats and how much.

Do not free feed (leave dry food out at all times) with a Pug and absolutely do not allow them to beg or get used to human food. Pugs get fat very quickly and it's difficult to pull the weight back off their compact, muscular bodies. You must feed Pugs at regular meal times with carefully measured servings.

When it comes to what food to serve to your precious Pug, the choices seem endless. There is **no one best food,** because some dogs need higher fat and protein than others, and some prefer canned over dry.

While food manufacturers are out to maximize their profits, as a rule you usually get what you pay for. So a more expensive food is generally more likely to provide **better nutrition** for your Pug in terms of minerals, nutrients, and higher quality meats in comparison to a cheap one, which will most likely **contain a lot of grain.** Even today, there are far too many dog food choices that continue to have far more to do with being convenient for us humans to serve, than they do with being a well-balanced, healthy food choice for the dog.

We will help guide you through the maze of the supermarket shelves, but in order to choose the right food for your Pug, first it's important to understand a little bit about canine physiology and what Mother Nature intended when she created our furry companions.

While humans are omnivores who can derive energy from eating plants, our canine companions are **natural carnivores,** which means they derive their energy and nutrient requirements from eating a diet consisting mainly or exclusively of the flesh of animals, birds, or fish — this provides proteins. Yes, proteins can be obtained from non-meat sources, but these are generally harder for the body to digest and have a higher chance of causing dietary intolerances.

Although dogs **can survive** on an omnivorous diet, this **does not mean** it is the best diet for them. Unlike humans, who are equipped with wide, flat molars for grinding grains, vegetables, and other plant-based materials, canine teeth are all pointed because they are designed to rip, shred, and tear into meat and bone.

Dogs are also born equipped with powerful jaws and neck muscles for the specific purpose of being able to pull down and tear apart their hunted prey. The structure of the jaw of every canine is such that it opens widely to hold large pieces of meat and bone, while the mechanics of a dog's jaw permits only vertical (up and down) movement that is designed for crushing.

The Canine Digestive Tract

A dog's digestive tract is short and simple and designed to move their natural choice of food (hide, meat, and bone) quickly through their system. Given the choice, most dogs would **never choose** to eat plants and grains, or vegetables and fruits over meat, however, we humans continue to feed them a kibble-based diet that contains high amounts of vegetables, fruits, and grains with low amounts of meat. Part of this is because we've been taught that it's a healthy, balanced diet for humans, and therefore, we believe that it must be the same for our dogs, and part of this is because all the fillers that make up our dog's food are less expensive and easier to process than meat.

While dogs can eat omnivorous foods, we are simply suggesting the **majority of their diet should consist of meats.**

One of the questions dog owners often ask is "Do dogs need fruits and vegetables?" In a 2006 committee on animal nutrition, the National Research Council (NRC) confirmed that dogs have **no nutritional requirements for carbohydrates.**

In their 2010 Pet Food Nutrient Profiles, the AAFCO concluded **carbohydrates are not essential to a healthy canine diet.**

But can plants play a role in supplementation? Many believe that **yes, plants can be a healthful addition** to the modern dog's diet and that vegetables provide essential nutrients, including fiber, minerals, and vitamins that an all-meat diet lacks. Advocates note that modern, intensive agricultural methods have stripped increasing amounts of nutrients from the soil. Crops grown decades ago (and the animals that ate them) were much richer in vitamins, minerals, and other nutrients than most of the varieties we get today.

Whatever you decide to feed your dog, keep in mind that just as too much wheat, other grains, and fillers in our human diet are having a detrimental effect on our health, the same can be very true for our best furry friends. Our dogs are also suffering from many of the same life-threatening diseases that are rampant in our **human society** as a direct result of consuming a diet high in genetically altered, impure, processed, and packaged foods.

Top Feeding Tips

High-quality dog foods provide all the nutrients, vitamins, minerals, and calories that your dog needs. This makes it a lot easier than our human diet where we have to make sure we eat many varieties of foods, and even then, we may be deficient in an important mineral or vitamin. But a word of warning: just because a food is branded as "premium" **doesn't mean it is.** The word is meaningless marketing.

Before buying any dog food, read the label. The first (main ingredient by weight) listed ingredients **should be a meat** such as beef, chicken, lamb, or fish.

Foods with large amounts of fillers like cornmeal or meat by-products have a **low nutritional value.** They fill your dog up, but don't give him the necessary range of vitamins and minerals, and they increase daily waste produced.

If grains are used, look for **whole grains** (i.e., whole grain corn, whole grain barley) and not cheaper by-products (corn gluten meal, soybean meal).

High-end premium diets avoid grains altogether in favor of carbohydrates such as white or sweet potato.

Avoid artificial colors like Erythrosine, also known as Red No. 3, preservatives such as BHA, BHT, Ethoxyquin, and sweeteners such as sucrose or high fructose corn syrup. Cut out sugars and salt.

AAFCO, the Association of American Feed Control Officials., develops guidelines for the production, labeling, and sale of animal foods. Choose a diet that complies with AAFCO specifications and conducts feeding trials. The label will say: Animal feeding tests using AAFCO procedures substantiate that (name of product) provides complete and balanced nutrition.

Grain-free (or raw) is often recommended for the Pug. Many are **allergic** to corn starch, wheat, and other grains. In addition, no soy should be in the dog food—it irritates them!

Wet foods are not appropriate for most growing dogs. They do not offer a good nutritional balance, and they are often upsetting to the stomach. Additionally, it's much harder to control portions with wet food, leading to young dogs being overfed or underfed.

If your Pug does not eat all of its meal in one go, you may be offering it too much. Many owners ask how many times a day they should feed, and the reality is it doesn't matter—what does is the correct feeding amount. You then divide this up by the number of meals you wish to serve. Most owners opt for twice a day for adult dogs.

Stools should be firm, dark brown, and crinkly if portions are correct. If they are firm but softer towards the end, this is an indication of overfeeding. Stools are an **indicator** of digestive upsets, if you notice they are runny or hard, there is a problem, as is excessive wind or an abnormal amount of feces. These should also not be brightly colored or smelly. Mucous in the stool is a common symptom of irritable bowel syndrome (IBS).

Invest in weighted food and water bowls made out of **stainless steel**. The weights prevent the mess of "tip overs," and the material is much easier to clean than plastic. It does not hold odors or harbor bacteria.

Bowls in a stand that create an **elevated feeding surface** are also a good idea. Make sure your young dog can reach the food and water. Stainless steel bowl sets retail for less than $25 / £15.

Julianne McCoy of Low Country Pugs: "I train all my Pugs to drink out of licker bottles which are made for canines which protects them from bacteria. They always have clean water."

Leave your Pug **alone** while it is eating from its bowl. Don't take the bowl away while he is eating. This causes anxiety, which can lead to **food aggression**.

Do you have more than one dog? I advise **feeding them separately** to completely avoid potential issues. One might try protecting his own food aggressively or try to eat the food designated for the other dog.

Feeding Your Puppy

As Pugs age, they thrive on a graduated program of nutrition. Up to the age of four months, puppies should get **four small meals** a day. From age four to eight months, **three meals** per day are appropriate. From eight months on, feed your Pug **twice** a day and consider switching to an adult formula.

TIP: From the very beginning of weaning, I put my hands into the puppies' bowls and feed them from my hands. I will take the food bowl from them and immediately offer them a tasty treat, then return their bowl. All of this teaches the puppy it is okay for hands to be around their food. I feel this is a very important life lesson where children are involved. Also, if a puppy grabs something that is not safe for them, they are much more willing to relinquish it.

Pugs will eat pretty much anything and everything put in front of them, so it is up to you to control their portions!

I highly recommend feeding puppies and dogs in the crate/kennel.

Begin feeding your puppy by putting the food down for 10–20 minutes. If the dog doesn't eat, or only eats part of the serving, still **take the bowl up**. Don't give the dog more until the next feeding time. Scheduled feedings in measured amounts are the preferred option and are less likely to lead to a fussy eater.

To give your puppy a good start in life, rely on high-quality, premium dry puppy food. If possible, replicate the puppy's existing diet. A sudden **dietary switch** can cause gastrointestinal upset, as puppies have sensitive stomachs. Take your pup to the vet if he has diarrhea or he has been vomiting for 48 hours or more.

Maintain the dog's existing routine if practical. To make an effective food transition, mix the existing diet with the new food, slowly changing the percentage of new to old over a period of ten days.

Some breeders recommend not using puppy food. It can be high in protein and actually can cause the puppy to **grow too fast**, thus possibly creating bone growth issues. You may want to switch to a junior or adult food once he leaves puppyhood. Your vet will help decide when best to switch.

Adult Nutrition

The same basic nutritional guidelines apply to adult Pugs. Always start with a high-quality, premium food. If possible, stay in the same product line the puppy received at the breeder. Graduated product lines help owners to create feeding programs that ensure nutritional consistency. This approach allows you to transition your Pug away from puppy food to an adult mixture, and in time, to a senior formula. This removes the guesswork from nutritional management.

Pugs should be fed **at least** twice a day to avoid bloat, which can be fatal. You should also **avoid exercise** immediately before or after eating.

Dogs don't make it easy to say no when they beg at the table. If you let a Pug puppy have so much as that first bite, you've created a little monster — and one with an unhealthy habit. As well as begging, this encourages drooling and negative attention-seeking behavior such as barking.

Never Feed These to Your Pug

Table scraps contribute to weight problems, and many human foods are toxic to dogs. They may be too rich for your Pug and cause him to scratch. Dangerous (some potentially fatal) items include:

- Chocolate
- Raisins and grapes
- Alcohol
- Human vitamins (especially those with iron)
- Mushrooms
- Garlic
- Onions
- Walnuts
- Macadamia nuts

Also, avoid sausage meat and cooked manufactured meats, as they can contain sulphite preservatives that can be harmful.

Never feed your Pug **cooked bones**, as these can splinter and cause internal damage or become an intestinal obstruction. If you give your puppy a bone, watch him. Use only bones that are too large to choke on and take the item away at the first sign of splintering. Commercial chew toys rated "puppy safe" are a much better option.

The Dehydrated Diet (Freeze-dried)

Dehydrated dog food comes in both raw and cooked forms, and these foods are usually air-dried to reduce moisture to the level where bacterial growth is inhibited.

The appearance of dehydrated dog food is very similar to dry kibble, and the typical feeding methods include adding warm water before serving, which makes this type of diet both healthy for our dogs and convenient for us to serve.

Dehydrated recipes are made from minimally processed fresh, whole foods to create a healthy and nutritionally balanced meal that will meet or exceed the dietary requirements for healthy canines. Dehydrating removes only the moisture from the fresh ingredients, which usually means that because the food has not already been cooked at a high temperature, more of the overall nutrition is retained.

A dehydrated diet is a convenient way to feed your dog a nutritious diet, because all you have to do is add warm water and wait five minutes while the food rehydrates so your Pug can enjoy a warm meal. There are, however, some potential disadvantages. It is **more expensive** than other diets (you are paying for the convenience factor), and because of the processing it can also **contain more preservatives** than you might ideally want.

Kibble Diet or Canned Food?

While many canine guardians are starting to take a closer look at the food choices they are making for their furry companions, there is no mistaking that the convenience and relative economy of dry dog food kibble, which had its beginnings in the 1940s, continues to make it the most popular dog-food choice for most humans. It is basically one of the least expensive choices and is quick, easy, and convenient to serve.

Dry kibble dog food is less messy than canned, easier to measure, and  can sit out all day without going bad. It is more economical per pound and is more energy-dense than canned food. This is because dry food is usually only 10% water, compared with about 75% water in cans. It takes a much larger volume of canned food to supply the nutrients your dog needs, as a can effectively only has 25% food. You are also likely to have to put half-finished cans in your fridge to keep them from going off, and they cause a strong smell which is unpleasant to some.

Be wary of cheap kibble, which often has high grain content and **is a false economy**, as they have to eat a lot to be well-nourished. Critics suggest that there is a lot of undercooked starch in dry dog food that can lead to gut problems: wind, loose stools, itchy skin, and fungal problems.

Canned food diets do have some **advantages**. Food manufacturers artificially boost the taste appeal of dry kibble by coating it with tempting fats, gravy, and other flavorings. In comparison, the wet and moist food fresh out of a can is much more edible to your Pug and often contains more protein, fat, and less additives and preservatives. The texture and smell also have added appeal to their senses!

The BARF/Raw Diet

Raw feeding advocates believe that the ideal diet for their dog is one that would be very similar to what a dog living in the wild would have access to, and these canine guardians are often opposed to feeding their dog any sort of commercially manufactured pet foods.

On the other hand, those opposed to feeding their dogs a raw or Biologically Appropriate Raw Food (BARF) diet believe that the risks associated with food-borne illnesses during the handling and feeding of raw meats outweigh the purported benefits.

A typical BARF diet is made up of 60–80% of crushed raw meaty bones (RMB). This is bones with about 50% meat, (e.g., chicken neck, back, and wings) and 20–40% of fruit and vegetables, offal, meat, eggs, or dairy foods.

Many owners directly oversee the raw diets, which usually consist of raw meat and bones, with some vegetables, fruits, supplements, and added grains.

Alternatively, you can buy commercial raw diet meals, which come either fresh or frozen. These supply all of the dog's requirements and are usually in a meat patty form. Always defrost it in the fridge, use what you need, and store the remainder on the bottom shelf of the fridge to use at the next mealtime, for up to four days.

Avoid feeding pork to your dog—eating raw or undercooked pork is not safe for dogs or humans due to the parasite *Trichinella spiralis* larvae, which can cause the trichinosis infection. Even if cooked, pork is rich with a type of fat that is difficult for them to digest, which can lead to indigestion and inflammation of the pancreas.

It is recommended that beef should be frozen before feeding, because of the Neospora intestinal parasite which can be found in cattle.

Many owners and breeders agree that their dogs thrive on a raw or BARF diet and strongly believe that the potential benefits of feeding a dog a raw food diet are many, including:

- Healthy, shiny coats
- Decreased shedding
- Fewer allergy problems
- Healthier skin
- Cleaner teeth
- Fresher breath
- Higher energy levels
- Improved digestion
- Smaller stools
- Strengthened immune system
- Increased mobility in arthritic pets
- General increase or improvement in overall health
- Ability to control what is in your Pug's food bowl
- Ability to avoid ingredients they are allergic or intolerant to
- No preservatives or additives

All dogs, whether working breed or lapdogs, are amazing athletes in their own right and deserve to be fed the best food available. A raw diet is a direct evolution of what dogs ate before they became our domesticated pets and when we turned toward commercially prepared, easy-to-serve dry dog food that required no special storage or preparation.

Many owners have reported seeing dogs plagued by chronic conditions such as atopy, obesity, and allergies, regaining their health after making the switch over to raw. The diet is low in carbs and free from grains, which turn directly into sugar in the body leading to fat deposition, and high in protein and fat.

A balanced raw diet naturally contains everything your dog could need nutritionally in an easily absorbable natural form. This means they won't seek out other food because of a deficiency. In addition, it also keeps them occupied for longer, so they are more likely to realize they're sated, and as they chew bones or chunks of meat, endorphins are released making them feel happier.

This all sounds good, doesn't it? So what **are the possible downsides?**

- Can be time consuming — less convenient.
- More expensive than other diets.
- Diet may not be balanced unless you are very careful — your Pug may become deficient in minerals and vitamins.
- Raw vegetables are often poorly digested by dogs.
- Safety for the elderly and young children —raw diets have been found to contain *Salmonella, Campylobacter, E. coli, Clostridium perfringens, Clostridium botulinium,* and *Staphylococcus aureus.* These are all known human and canine pathogens.
- Safety to your Pug—some raw foods contain pathogens which can make your dog very sick (even fatally) such as *Neospora caninum,* found in raw beef, *Nanophyetus salmincola,* found in raw salmon, and *Trichinella spiralis,* found in raw pork.

Raw food advocates simply suggest that you use common-sense practices such as washing your hands after handling raw food and cleaning your knives, chopping boards, and surfaces, either in the dishwasher or in hot soapy water. You can also put your Pug's bowl in the dishwasher, which will kill bacteria.

If you can't feed your Pug a raw diet for whatever reason, please think enough of him or her to at least feed a topical enzyme/probiotic so they can process their food better. These can help your dog with weight loss because a healthy gut means healthy digestion. Some naturally probiotic-rich foods are sauerkraut, kimchi, kefir, and live yoghurt (goat or sheep dairy is always better than cow).

TIP: Add some Psyllium Husk Fibre to the raw food. This expands in the stomach, leaving your Pug feeling fuller and acts as a prebiotic. Not to be confused with probiotics; **prebiotics** stimulate the growth of friendly bacteria in the large intestine.

TIP: Organ tissues such as beef and bison liver provide essential amino acids necessary to supply your Pug's high protein needs. Liver is one of the most nutrient-rich foods containing vitamin A, all B vitamins, D, and important minerals such as iron, phosphorus, and copper.

Raw feeding can be cheaper than dried food. While there are some ready-prepared and pre-packaged raw foods which may be quite costly it is also possible to do very basic raw food, i.e. meat and mixer, and this is definitely cheaper than dried and in my opinion, is better for your Pugs.

Food Allergies

Unfortunately, just like humans, Pugs sometimes react badly to certain foods. It is important to look out for signs, especially itchy skin, but also rubbing of the face on the floor or carpet, excessive scratching, ear infections, hot patches, and rash on the chin and face.

The most **common allergies** are to beef, dairy products, chicken, wheat, eggs, corn starch, and soy. As with any allergy, remove suspect items or try a special diet. Helpful **supplements** include quercetin, bromelain and papain, diffused eucalyptus oil, and local honey.

Pugs need diversity in their diets just like humans do, and if he has been eating the same food for months he may have grown sensitive to certain allergenic ingredients, typically grains and other carbohydrates. Even the protein might be at fault because this is often laced with antibiotics and hormones causing overreaction in the immune system.

Allergy testing offers a definitive diagnosis and pinpoints necessary environmental and dietary changes. The tests are expensive, costing about $200+ / £120+.

Work with your vet to develop an allergy elimination diet to help identify the source of the issue. Then new foods are added back in one at a time to gauge your dog's reaction and response. They may also suggest natural supplements to help with detoxifying the immune system.

How Much to Feed?

There is no definite answer because it depends on a number of varying factors. **Your Pug is unique.** Even with two the same age, they can have differing metabolic levels, with one being very energetic compared to the other, which might be a slouch!

The amount of daily exercise you are able to give your Pug is a critical factor because they will burn off more calories the more they do and thus, can eat more without putting on weight.

As a general rule, smaller Pugs have faster metabolisms so require a higher amount of food per pound of body weight. Younger Pugs also need more food than seniors, who by that age have a slower metabolic rate.

The type of food you serve is also a factor. There are definitely some lesser quality (low-priced) foods that may have the weight (bulk) but offer less in terms of nutrition and goodness.

Be slightly cynical when reading the recommended daily allowance on the labels because they are usually higher than need be. Remember this is from the manufacturer who profits the more your Pug eats!

Treats

These are a great way to reward your Pug for good behavior and also for training purposes. However there are some precautions to note. Many are **high in sugar** and can contain artificial additives, milk, and fat.

Good quality treats can have nutritional value, but you really don't want to overuse them; I suggest they make up a maximum of 15% of the dog's total daily calorie intake. Try to use **praise as a reward** instead, so you are not always using treats every time he needs rewarding.

Don't forget that treats don't just come out of a packet or box, they can also include normal items such as steamed vegetables, apple slices, and carrot sticks.

A great way to reward and stimulate your Pug is a toy that dispenses the treat (food) when he works a puzzle out. The best-known is perhaps the Kong. This chew toy is made of nearly indestructible rubber. Kong sells specially shaped treats and different things you can squeeze inside, but you can stuff it with whatever your Pug likes best.

Nina Ottosson is a genius Swedish pioneer in the world of interactive dog puzzle toys. Her offerings come in a variety of levels of difficulty and in both plastic and wood.

TIP: Take a hot dog, cut it into fourths along its length and then chop the long, skinny lengths into lots of little pieces. Cook in the microwave for at least two minutes longer than you would normally cook a hot dog. You should have 50 + pieces to use as rewards.

Some people like to fill toys with treats such as peanut butter but be aware of "low sugar" or "no sugar" peanut butters. They often replace the sugar with the artificial sweetener Xylitol, which is toxic to dogs. Look for ones with no added sweeteners or salt. Ingredients should state 100% peanuts.

Ingredients — Be Careful!

Learning what the labels mean on the back of packaging is really important to understand the quality of food you are giving to your beloved Pug.

Some manufacturers can use cute tricks to **disguise** the amount of grains in their product. They list them separately (to push them down the list order) but added together they can add up to a sizeable amount.

The reverse is true, where they add all the meat ingredients together as one so it appears as the first listed ingredient — but check what else the food consists of!

Although milk contains several beneficial nutrients, it also contains a high proportion of sugar lactose. As in humans, many dogs have **real difficulties digesting** lactose and as a result, milk products can bring on stomach pains, flatulence, diarrhea, and even vomiting.

When you see meat listed, this refers to the clean flesh of slaughtered animals (chicken, cattle, lamb, turkey, etc.). The flesh can include striated skeletal muscle, tongue, diaphragm, heart, esophagus, overlying fat and the skin, sinew, nerves, and blood vessels normally found with that flesh.

When you see meat by-products listed, this refers to the clean parts of slaughtered animals, not including meat. These include lungs, spleen, kidneys, brain, liver, blood, bone, some fatty tissue, and stomach and intestines freed of their contents (it doesn't include hair, horns, teeth, or hooves).

Don't mistake dry food as being very low in meat content compared to wet food that lists fresh meat as an ingredient. Fresh meat consists of two-thirds water, so you need to discount the water when doing your comparisons between the two.

The **Guaranteed Analysis** on the label is very helpful, as it contains the exact percentages of crude protein, fat, fiber, and moisture.

Don't be scared off if the main ingredient is chicken meal rather than fresh beef. This is simply chicken that is dehydrated, and it contains more protein than fresh chicken, which is 80 percent water. The same is true for beef, fish, and lamb.

Look out for Sodium Tripolyphosphate (E451), an artificial preservative historically used as a component of detergents and other industrial products shown to cause vomiting.

Potassium Sorbate (E202) is an irritant that damages skin, eyes, and

in preparing the full portion meal, mix a half-portion of your dog food and a half-portion size of canned, unsalted, green beans. Green beans will act as a filler but won't cause weight gain. Never feed green beans alone, as the dog will not receive proper nutrition. Also, instead of a full treat, give him half a treat ... he doesn't measure! This will cut his food in half without him starving. Don't rely on your Pug to stop eating when he is full! No, they will eat anything they see in front of them just because it's available!

Avoid genetically engineered, carb-loaded, and chemically laced foods. A high-fat, low-to-moderate protein, ultra-low-carb diet is best for your Pug. Dogs (and cats) have NO requirement to intake starch (aka sugar). They can thrive with no carbohydrates in their diet, yet the average pet food ranges from 30 percent to 70 percent carbs!

Natural Medicines—Herbs for a Healthy Diet

Herbal medicine is the oldest recorded form of medicine, involving the use of plants or their extracts as medicine. Before they were used for medicine, plants were used as food for flavor and nutrition. Now most food comes in packaging, ready-made or processed with sugar and salt and other additives used for flavor.

Instead, why not try adding some herbs to your Pug's diet? Parsley, basil, mint, oregano, sage, rosemary, and thyme are aromatic and flavor-filled because of their volatile oil components. Freshly chopped or dried, they can be added to meals every day, using anywhere from a pinch to a teaspoon, depending on your dog's size and health.

Spices and seeds often used in Eastern cooking such as turmeric, ginger, fennel seed, cayenne, and cinnamon all have health benefits. These are most commonly added to food as powders, although turmeric and ginger can be used fresh, and fennel seed is often made into a tea.

Feeding Older Pugs

Once your Pug passes the age of eight, he can be considered a "senior," and his body has different requirements than those of a young dog. You may notice signs of your dog slowing down, putting on weight, or having joint issues. This is the time to discuss and involve your vet in considering switching to a senior diet.

Because his body's metabolism is slowing down, the adult diet he is on may have too many calories that **cannot be burned off** with the amount of exercise he is capable of. This isn't your fault, so don't feel guilty.

Don't let the pounds pile on. They are much harder to take off than put on, and his weight will **literally affect his longevity**, as more strain is being put on his internal organs and joints. Senior diets are specially formulated to have a lower calorie count. They tend to be higher in fiber to prevent constipation, which senior dogs can be prone to.

Some breeders also suggest supplements such as glucosamine and chondroitin, which assist joints.

The opposite problem to weight gain is loss of appetite. It may be as simple as needing a change of food, but it could be issues with his teeth. A moister food may help, but first get his teeth checked by your vet.

A breeder friend of mine told me of his aging dogs barking for no apparent reason. He started feeding them Pro Plan Bright Minds and saw a difference for the better within a few weeks. He says they are more alert and the barking for no apparent reason just stopped.

What the Breeders Advise on Feeding and Diet

Felicity Prideaux of Hugapug: "I am a passionate raw feeder. And have been for over 10 years. Those of us who are of the "baby boomers" generation remember how healthy the family pets were—fed on meat and offal lots of bones, and leftover cooked vegetables and whatever fruit they stole off the fruit trees in the back yard—everything packed full of nature's goodness!

"Then we introduced to our happy little pets, highly processed food with loads of preservatives, fillers, cereals and artificial vitamins. Overtime it became evident that our wonderful companions were getting health issues, skin problems and dental issues being most prevalent.

"Fortunately, over the last 25 years or so there has been a recognition that raw feeding is actually great for your dogs! Let's face it, kibble isn't very palatable—I know, I've tried it! How would you like to have the same dry and not very exciting food every meal! I know I wouldn't and neither would my fussy Pugs!

"In the morning I feed a variety of human grade raw meat (beef, chicken, lamb and kangaroo) from Platinum K9 Industries mixed with a specially prepared grain free raw additive called InnerWinner which includes alfalfa, chia seed, gentian, kelp, st marys thistle, garlic, celery, pea, protein, molasses, livermol, sunflower and coconut. I regularly add whole chicken hearts to the mix.

"At night it is bones or chicken or salmon frames—but always something that they have to work to eat. My puppies are fed raw from weaning and they are fed a variety of different meats, vegetables and fruits as well as goat's milk and goat's milk yoghurt."

Michele Bearden of Charmin Pugs: "We use Fromm Salmon Ala Veg, we also add a Fromm Can with this: Pups three to four times a day until six months and they eat the Puppy No Grain by Fromm."

Lundi Blamey of Claripugs: "If one wants to be diligent about this topic then read the labels to find out what is in the food. The companies that manufacture kibble will likely add filler so read the label. Make note of the protein concentration in the food along with what other ingredients are included. Ingredients such as "animal by-products" tell you nothing about what is actually present in the food that you feed your pet.

"My Pugs get a mixture of kibble and raw food. Using a heavy duty grinder, we typically grind raw chicken backs, beef heart, and organ meat, along with vegetables such as kale, parsley, pumpkin and mixed berries. A small amount of kelp and minerals is added. Diatomaceous Earth can periodically be added as a worm preventative. The mixture is then put into freezer bags and frozen for later use. Grinding 30 kg of food in one sitting is our norm but if you are feeding only one Pug, then a large quantity will probably be too much and therefore speak to your butcher about what they can get for you. When asked why add organ meat, I draw owners attention to the fact that predators in the wild will eat the organs first to get the nutrients. One note of caution, however, I have heard of some owners encountering issues by feeding raw chicken necks, however, we do not feed necks. The formula can be easily changed for your individual dog.

"Some people ask why do I feed raw? There are some advantages. My Pugs do not have dental issues on a raw food diet. Our vet will examine their mouths and comment that there is no tartar buildup on their teeth. Even our nine-year old does not have dental issues. We also find that the motions are better. Over the years we have seen that a dog with loose motions on being fed a raw chicken wing will recover from diarrhea within a day. Our Pugs love their raw food and by feeding the raw, it is an easy way to include a tablet which would otherwise be a dramatic event to get the tablet down their throat. Another form of raw food that Pugs enjoy is rough tripe. Many pet stores will carry frozen tripe or else ask your local butcher.

"So what about a bone? Our Pugs love a beef marrow bone of the right size that has been cooked for half an hour in an oven. It keeps them busy and the bone helps to clean their teeth. We never feed mature chicken bones whereas a young immature chicken has soft bones and the Pugs can munch these bones without the bones splintering.

"Be sensible about what your Pug eats. A wedge of apple is always appreciated and six to ten blue berries can be used as treats or rewards."

TIP: Great natural treats—CARROTS. They serve to help keep dogs' teeth clean and are much healthier for them than commercial biscuits, etc. Dogs LOVE them! Our grocery store sells 15-pound bags for $10. Economical, healthy treat!

TIP: For puppy upset stomachs—keep a can of pure pumpkin on hand, not the pie mix, but pure pumpkin. Give a tablespoon on top of dry food, once a day. Alternate this with a tablespoon of plain yogurt the next day. This is great for stomach/digestive problems.

Managing Your Pug's Activity

Pugs love being exercised. In addition to taking your Pug for long walks—plan on incorporating hearty games of fetch, runs, and hikes into your dog's life: The more activity the better. These outings not only keep your dog's body in good shape, they stimulate his mind.

Many owners ask if Pugs can swim, while technically yes they can, they are poor swimmers and I wouldn't advise to encourage this.

Food is a powerful motivator for a real "chow hound" like a Pug. Hiding and sniffing out treats provide these dogs with endless entertainment. It's all a treasure hunt as far as your pet is concerned.

Seize every opportunity to get your dog outdoors and doing something to avoid problem behaviors, separation anxiety, and destruction caused by the simple fact that the poor dog is bored out of his mind.

Your Pug likes routine, so establish one and stick to it as much as possible. Just because you have a garden or yard does not mean that you don't need to walk your dog. He needs mental stimulation as well as physical.

Note that, when Pugs are young, exercise should be limited in as much as pounding pavements should be avoided. I think it is imperative not to over-exercise puppies under six months. I have seen baby puppies end up as adults with very unsound joints, as they have been taken for too many long walks. Young puppies have soft

bones/joints like a child, and they don't really firm up until they are five to six months old. Over-exercising can upset the growth plates, which can cause weakness in the elbows, pasterns, and stifles.

Free running for short bursts of a few minutes at a time is fine, and as the puppy reaches around six months, the periods of free running can be increased. The general rule which I like is five to ten minutes per month of age in young puppies for exercise. So a pup which has just finished vaccinations would get 15–30 minutes vigorous exercise a day maximum. Remember as well that this includes playing chase games around the house. Too much exercise and your Pug puppy will end up with fine bones and leggy, as they only grow when asleep.

Once muscles and bones are fully grown when the dog is around twelve months, they can really take as much exercise as the owner wants to give. This should be on a daily basis and not confined to weekends!

Pugs are intelligent and need mental stimulation in addition to physical training, and may become fractious if their lifestyle is too sedentary.

As a rule of thumb, around **half an hour free running daily** when they are adults will be enough to keep your Pug toned, and this coupled with a good-sized garden to patrol will keep him on his toes.

Annie Sullivan of CASull Pugs: "Pugs up until they're about two to three years old have a lot of energy if they don't get the proper exercise. They need room to run and play. After about three years they're happy to just be a couch potato. When I asked my mentors if fawns were different to blacks they said "Oh YES they are! Fawns think they know everything but a black KNOWS they know everything!"

Pugs and Heat

Pugs don't cope well with heat due to their shortened nose and less breathing room so you must consider summer temperatures—your Pug also has a fur coat it can't take off, and it doesn't have the same cooling-down options available to us. If you feel you are too hot or start to sweat, then don't walk your dog at that time of day; early mornings and evenings are the best time. **Always** make sure that you have water available if you go out for a walk.

TIP: Think about hot sidewalks (pavements). Before a walk, place the back of your hand on the ground and hold it there. If you cannot hold it there for a minute, then it is too hot for your Pug. Their paws are extremely sensitive and can get burned or even stick to tarmac or other hard surfaces in hot weather.

Consider car journeys and heat and never leave them unattended as they could easily suffer heat stroke where their soft palate swells and blocks the airways. You need to remain as calm as you can while bringing their temperature down rapidly.

Ideas for cooling them down include: having a paddling pool, hosing or

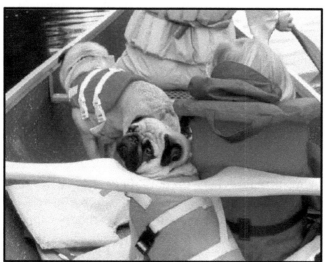

sponging them down, or providing a fan near them (a wet towel placed in front of the fan adds a bit of moisture to the air as an added bonus).

Photo Credit: Doris Klingbeil of Gibby Pugs.

Collar or Harness?

Some breeders are fans of using a traditional collar, some prefer harnesses that look like vests. They offer a point of attachment for the lead on the back between the shoulders. This arrangement directs pressure away from the neck and allows for easy, free movement. Young dogs are less resistant to this system and don't strain against a harness the way they will with a collar.

It's best to take your Pugs with you to the pet store to get a proper fit. Sizing for a dog is much more unpredictable than you might think. Regardless of size, harnesses retail in a range of about $20–$25 / £12–£15.

Julianne McCoy of Low Country Pugs: "In the US it is recommended to forego putting a collar on a Pug and instead to put on a soft harness to protect the skin around the Pugs neck. A harness or collar with a rabies tag should be visible at any dog park and a Pug must be spayed or neutered before taking inside of a dog park."

Standard Leash or Retractable?

The decision to buy a standard, fixed-length leash or a retractable lead is, for the most part, a matter of personal preference. Some facilities like groomers, vet clinics, and dog daycares ask that you not use a retractable lead on their premises. The long line represents a trip and fall hazard for other human clients.

Fixed-length leashes often sell for as little as $5 / £3, while retractable leads are less than $15 / £9.

Learning to respond to your control of the leash is an important behavioral lesson for your Pug. Do not **drag** a Pug on a lead or **jerk him**. If he sits down and refuses to budge, pick him up. Don't let the dog be in charge of the walk or you'll have the devil's own time regaining the upper hand.

Pugs love to get out in the world and "sniff the trail." They will associate the lead with adventures and time with you. Don't be at all surprised if your dog picks up words associated with excursions like go, out, car, drive, or walk and responds accordingly.

Pug Walking Tips

Active dogs like Pugs are into the whole walking experience. This is an excellent opportunity to use the activity to build and reinforce good behaviors on command.

Teach your Pug to sit by using the word and making a downward pointing motion with your finger or indicating the desired direction with the palm of your hand. Do not attach the lead until your dog complies, rewarding his patience with the words he most wants to hear: "Okay, let's go!"

If your Pug jerks or pulls on the leash, stop and only walk on again when the puppy has returned to you. Or turn and walk the other way. Puppies quickly learn pulling means no walking and will walk quietly at your side.

Praise your Pug for walking well on the end of the lead and for stopping when you stop. Reinforce positive behaviors during walks. Your dog will get the message and show the same traits during other activities.

If you have a reluctant puppy try using a small treat in your hand to encourage him to walk forward on a lead.

Pugs and Activities

Jim Bradley of Joie De Vivre Pugs: "Rally obedience is a sport ideal for Pugs to start their performance careers. Rally provides an opportunity to compete against other dogs on a course with between 10 to 20 stations. Each station has a sign which tells the handler the skill to be performed and follows a pattern and sequence designed by the judge. Stations are grouped by level and as you successfully complete the

skills starting in Novice you can move up to a more challenging level. Beginning levels are on-lead and advanced levels are off-lead.

Photo Credit: Jim Bradley of Joie De Vivre Pugs - Trax in 'front' position looking up at me to see what he is expected to do next.

"Where Rally obedience differentiates from traditional obedience is in formality. In Rally you are encouraged to talk to your Pug during the entire performance. Rally is casual, fun, and with a Pug, entertaining. This is not to say Rally is not challenging, it is, but it also builds on the bond between you and your Pug as you continue to train and compete.

"Many competitors start in Rally and move to Obedience and Agility, as well as other sports. These companion sports provide the opportunity to extend the skills learned in Rally. The essence of Rally is fun. When competing in any sport remember your Pug is a natural clown. No matter how well trained your Pug is this humorous characteristic will emerge at some time while competing. These are the most memorable and wonderful moments."

"Pugs do really well in obedience, rally and agility but they also do well in coursing, freestyle, tracking, and other dog-related activities. There are also a number of other organizations other than the AKC that offer similar venues, especially in agility. They say Pugs are hard to train— obviously the person saying this did not have food in their hand."

Pam Donaldson of Highland/Kendoric Pugs: "Contrary to their history of stubbornness, and difficulty staying on a task oriented to obedience, Pugs are not devoid of smarts. They love activities that pique their interest and can be very enthusiastic doing agility. I have yet to have a Pug of mine not go behind a mirror or the TV to find what was making that image they see and this is seen as a test of intelligence. They always know where the food is, and they quickly adapted to the sound my cell phone makes when it notifies me that my camera has picked up someone at the front door."

Dr. Jeff and Amy McLelland of Pickwick Pugs: "Every Pug we have owned has been intelligent. In fact, my husband and I were surprised when we realized that our very first Pug had learned to identify specific toys ("pig", "cow", "ball") entirely on her own without any training on our part. The judges at AKC Rally Obedience trials always seem surprised when our Pug, Sebastian BGR, CGC, RN, RA walks away with the blue ribbons, beating out the more biddable dogs such as Border Collies and Golden Retrievers. These biddable dogs often earn the reputation of being the most intelligent breeds, however, in our opinion, the fact that Pugs will not simply comply to a command barked out by his owner only proves their extreme intelligence. Pugs prefer to figure things out for themselves and they do not thrive in a "dictatorship environment." While our Retriever mix prefers to simply be told what to do, and will willingly repeat the task over and over for a simple pat on the head or a smile, our Pugs prefer "shaping techniques" which afford them the freedom to think for themselves. The Pugs will also require a detailed itinerary of the specific rewards

they will be receiving, present and future. Our Pugs generally figure out a new skill with a few tries while the Labrador and Retriever mixes tend to require a few days of repetition before the light bulb goes off. However, the Pugs will require days, weeks, months, (years?!) of "proofing" and will need a much wider learning curve since they are constantly reinventing the rules and reward-requirements for completing the given task. While some Pugs are more biddable than others, they all seem to abide by the same motto: "If it's not fun and rewarding, we are checking out!"

Playtime and Toys

Pugs are smart, so give your dog plenty of toys, and observe what he does and doesn't like to do. You'll know soon enough if he's willing to learn tricks with you.

In obedience training, your Pug will learn a basic set of commands like sit, stay, and heel. These commands can be used as the basis to get your dog to respond to cues to perform tricks, but only if he is agreeable. There's no guarantee your Pug will cooperate. He may just walk away. It doesn't hurt to try, but never try to force your pet to do something he really doesn't want to do.

Always offer praise and show pleasure for correct responses. This makes training just another form of play—and **Pugs love to play**!

The speed with which your dog will amass and destroy a collection of toys may shock you. Avoid soft rubber toys—they shred into small pieces, which the dog will swallow. Opt for rope toys instead, or chew toys that can withstand the abuse. You can buy items made out of this tough material in the $1–$5 / £0.60–£3.00 range. Don't buy anything with a squeaker or any other part that presents a choking hazard.

Never give your dog rawhide or pig's ears, which soften and present a choking hazard although I do use cow's hooves. They soften well in the rain and Pugs love them. So far I have never seen them splinter.

Playtime is important, especially for a dog's natural desire to chase. Try channeling this instinct with toys and games. If a dog has no stimulation and has nothing to chase, he may start to chase his own tail, which could lead to problems. Dogs that don't get enough exercise are also more likely to develop problem behaviors like chewing, digging, and barking.

Toys can be used to simulate the dog's natural desire to hunt. For example, when they catch a toy, they will often shake it and bury their teeth into it, simulating the killing of their prey.

The cheap tunnels for children make good skills toys for puppies, as do Kong toys with dangling ends. For a new Pug puppy in his first home, stuffing a Kong with food and freezing it, makes a good toy to keep a puppy occupied whilst teaching being left for periods alone.

Allow your dog to fulfill **a natural desire** to chew. This comes from historically catching their prey and then chewing the carcass. Providing chews or bones can prevent your dog from destroying your home. Deer antlers are wonderful toys for a Pug; most love them but the dental vets hate them, as they believe they cause teeth fractures. They do not smell, are all-natural, and do not stain or splinter. I recommend the antlers that are not split; they last longer.

Playing with your dog is not only a great way of getting them to use up their energy, but it is also a **great way of bonding** with them as they have fun. Dogs love to chase and catch balls, but make sure that the ball is too large to be swallowed.

I also recommend having a toy mobile over the pen with various soft and hard toys hanging down, and I have a game that you hide food under and they have to move the pieces to get the food—great for making them use their senses. Puppies need to experience a variety of different textures, whether rubber, plastic, or soft fabrics.

Chapter 8 — Showing Your Pug

If you have purchased a show-quality Pug and are planning to enter the world of conformation dog shows and the dog fancy, you have a whole education in front of you. If you have not already done so, you will want to begin to attend dog shows and to make connections in the world of the dog fancy to acquire the training needed to participate with your Pug, or to hire someone to show the animal for you.

Firstly, talk to the breeder (who hopefully, is a person serious about Pugs). An experienced breeder will be happy to mentor you or suggest someone in your area who can give tips and advice. Finding a local ringcraft class for show people, will help with socializing with different breeds and also tips for showing.

Photo credit: Julia Ashton of Zobear Pugs.

If you might be interested in showing, always tell the breeder before purchasing a puppy, and they will then ensure you get a show-quality puppy (as far as one can tell at eight weeks). Also, be sure to buy from a kennel that does actually show on a regular basis.

The best thing you can do if you are planning to show your puppy is socializing them once they have settled in their new home. The work you put in at this stage of your puppy's life will shape them for life, so you need to get it right; take it slowly, and build it up gently. Remember they are only babies, and they need to know you are there for them and are in charge of every situation.

Your puppy needs to be happy for a judge to run their hands all over him, so it is very important to get him used to this. When your Pug puppy is happy for you to be able to touch them all over, you can get your trusted friends to do the same. Start at the head, look in their ears and eyes, and run your hands all down their back and down their legs.

What Dogs Are Qualified to Participate?

For a dog to participate in a dog show, it must be registered with the governing body for that exhibition. For instance, dogs registered with the American Kennel Club that are six months or older on the day of the show are eligible to enter AKC sponsored events. Spayed or neutered dogs are not eligible, nor are dogs with disqualifying faults according to the accepted standard for the breed. It's generally easier to show a male, as opposed to a female, because females can be hard on their coat and change behavior during their heat cycles.

Joining a Breed Club

When you attend a dog show, find out about joining a breed-specific club in your area. Such groups usually sponsor classes to teach the basics in handling and showing the breed or will have contacts to put you in touch with individual teachers.

Breed club membership is also important for learning the culture of the dog fancy and to meet people in the show world. You will begin by participating in smaller, local shows to learn the ropes before entering an event that will garner points toward sanctioned titles within a governing group's system.

There are also "fun matches" that a new dog owner can participate in, and which are open to dogs from three to six months of age. Here the owner can get an idea of how dog show judging takes place. It's also a great training ground for that future show prospect. The more you know about your breed, its care and maintenance, and the handling of them, the better you will be in the show ring. Study your country's parent kennel club's official breed standard.

Don't Be Put Off by Fear

My advice to folks who are interested in starting to show is go to several shows and watch the dogs in the ring. Talk to the folks at the sidelines; most are very happy to talk dogs with you.

Find a successful show person to evaluate the dog you plan to start showing. Although anybody can show a dog, you need to get an objective appraisal of your dog's qualities. To qualify as a show dog, it can't have any disqualifying faults, so it is important you find a mentor who can honestly help you evaluate your dog.

I also advise you to attend conformation classes in your area if possible, and be sure your dog is well-socialized. Most local Kennel Clubs offer these classes at very reasonable rates. Presentation and the dog's attitude are also very important factors. Shy and timid dogs usually don't do well at a dog show.

Don't forget that judges' assignments are to assess the breeding stock quality of the exhibits before them via the official breed standard description, observations on movement, and their hands-on experience. There are good judges and the opposite. Many owners have found that performance events, such as obedience, agility, rally, and therapy dog provide great satisfaction in lieu of conformation events.

Of course, you always hope your dog will win. If you have done all your homework, and your dog is a good representative of the breed, you should walk in the ring with confidence and present your dog as well as possible. There is no such thing as a perfect dog, and a good handler will know how to hide the faults and show off the best traits.

I always found going to a dog show exciting. You should always think of it as fun. It will give you an opportunity to meet many people who are also fanciers of your particular breed. Although it is a competition, whether you win or lose, you should always be a good sport. Remember, there will always be another show, another judge, and different competition. After a while, you will get to know which judges like a particular type or style of your breed.

Hiring a Professional

It is not uncommon for people who own show quality animals to hire professional handlers to work with the dogs. If you are interested in going this route, be sure to interview several handlers and to get a full rundown of their rates. Attend a show where they are working with a dog and watch them in action. Ask for references, and contact the people whose names you are given.

Entrusting a handler with the care of your dog is an enormous leap of faith. You want to be certain you have hired someone with whom you are completely comfortable and with whom your Pug has an observable rapport.

Tips and Advice

Stacking is how the dog stands naturally and when placed in position. This helps the judges see all areas of the dog's structure to evaluate against the breed standard and to allow the judges to feel the dogs bone structure and muscles.

Stand your puppy on a non-slip surface on a table. Front legs should be straight and parallel as should the hocks. Stack each leg individually with one hand. Front legs at the elbow and hind legs by the stifle. Stack the rear legs in line with the front legs.

The aim is to hold the puppy's head under the chin and make sure the tail is as curled as possible. Take care your puppy doesn't jump or fall off the table, as they can move very fast! You may find your puppy won't cooperate and refuses to be stacked. This is normal! Be confident, firm and tell him to stand.

Reward the puppy with praise and a treat only if he stacks. If he refuses, keep calm and put him on the floor without praise and try again later. The puppy will be less likely to stack if he is lively and energetic. Make it easier by waiting until he has tired a little.

He will soon learn what you want him to do. Start with very short periods, just a few seconds of stacking gradually increasing the time. It may seem as if he will never stack for you, but don't worry, one day he will suddenly do it! Once he is standing well on the table, also start standing him on the ground.

Be well-organized. Get to the show at least an hour before you are in the ring, as this will give you and your dog time to settle down.

Ensure you have your ring number on when you enter the ring. Make a strong entrance—you only get one chance to make an impression.

Remember, the judge will look across the ring from time to time, so have your dog facing the judge even when you are relaxed. Always keep an eye on the judge.

Before you set off, have your arm in an L shape. It will help you keep in a straight line and have more control. Look at something in front of you, keep your eyes on it, and move towards it. Say your dog's name, then say "move."

Never give treats when you are moving your dog, as your dog will look up at you, and you need it to go in a straight line. In addition, don't give treats when the judge is going over your dog. Save the treat your dog loves the most for shows, not training, so you can get their attention even more so.

Don't get boxed in a corner at the show; give yourself plenty of room by not standing too close to other exhibiters.

Always dress smartly, wear good shoes you can run in, and if you're a woman, wear a sports bra.

Hold your head up, and try to look confident and like a winner. The judge needs to know you can hold your own and show your dog off in the big ring. If you look too shy, they may think you are not up to the job of representing your breed in the group ring.

Always have a cloth to wipe your dog's mouth dry. Do this just before it's your turn to stand your dog for the judge. It makes showing the bite so much easier.

Warm your dog up before you go in the ring by having a little practice run.

Finally, always take your dog to show in good, clean condition.

Photo credit: SachiiPeace Photography & Felicity Prideaux of Hugapug.

Remember that it is also very competitive, and like all competitive endeavors, you'll find a wide range of personalities participating. Try to get to know the people who have a positive attitude and display good sportsmanship. Remember to always have fun with your dog; after all, he's your family's 'best in show' and he's doing his best to please you.

Julia Ashton of Zobear Pugs has enormous experience showing her Pugs notably winning at Crufts in 2015 where she won Best of Breed with her Pug Marbelton What a Guy and in 2017 she won Best of Breed at the World Dog Show. We asked Julia what advice would she offer regarding choosing the best possible Pug for chances of success?

"Wanting a show puppy, do plenty of research, visit shows and watch and learn. There are different types of Pug within the breed, which one is for you? You may need to wait for that show puppy but once you have, this is my advice on training and some tips. Take your young puppy everywhere, garden center, the shops, town center out in the car, when old enough walk out on busy roads. Get them used to all loud noises, go to puppy training classes, practice, practice, practice.

"Tips—have a friend photograph you when you think you've stacked your Pug, then look at the picture, are they stood full square, are the front legs straight and the back legs straight, is the top line straight? Keep doing this until without looking at your Pug you can stack them perfectly. If showing on the grass, make sure you are standing on level ground, make sure the grass is not long; these things can make your Pug either look sloped or short in leg. When showing, always have your Pug bathed, fit, and reasonably obedient for the ring. Take care of your own appearance, smart suit, hair neat, flat shoes, no dangling jewellery or long painted nails. Most of all enjoy your Pug, you take the best dog home and if you work hard you never know you might just win Best of Breed at Crufts!"

Jeanne Hilton Henderson of Hilton Kennels: "Pugs are groomed and shown on a table. Buy a grooming arm and noose for the neck for grooming or anything else if showing. They will not jump off the table easily and will face forward for easier grooming.

"When teaching the dog to stand on the table, stack each leg individually with one hand. Front legs at the elbow and hind legs by the stifle. Stack the rear legs in line with the front legs.

"Hiring a handler in the US is common for breeders who cannot travel to some shows as well as the new Pug owners.

"When entering the Pug in a show make sure the weight is good and the coat is in good condition. Toenails are trimmed and brush all the loose coat out so the judge doesn't get it on their hands."

The Westminster Dog Show and Crufts

So how does an owner get to take part in the famous Westminster Dog Show in the United States?

It is a requirement that in order to compete, your dog must already have earned a major toward its AKC championship or have an AKC championship. The entry forms are sent out in October of the previous year, and there is a limit to the number of entries that are accepted. This number has increased in the last few years, and most entries are now accepted if submitted properly within a few days of the first acceptance date in December.

Submit your entry online, USPS, or through a third-party entry service. In the past, it was more difficult to get your entry received before the limit was reached. Since the class judging moved from Madison Square Garden to the Piers it has become easier, as the limit is higher.

Dog shows are the second oldest sport, next to the Kentucky Derby. It is a great sport, where you can make wonderful friends, including from other countries. It can be a family affair; children can start to compete against each other in the junior classes as early as eight years old.

There is a significant difference between showing at an AKC show and showing at a Kennel Club show. Most AKC shows occur in just one day—Westminster being one of the exceptions—and the vast majority of shows are between 500–1000 dogs total. There are frequently multiple shows on consecutive days in the same venue, and the chance to win points at each event. If you are just getting started in the US, visit a show without entering. Many AKC shows have "Dog Show Tours" or will pair you with an experienced person if you are looking to get started. You can find more information about this on their website.

The world-famous Crufts show in the UK is the only show in the UK where dogs have to qualify to enter by having won at least a third place in their breed at another championship show in the preceding year. Despite being another show, Crufts has its own personality unlike any other event. The anticipation and the razzmatazz make it extra special.

There are plenty of shows apart from Crufts. If you think you might like to exhibit your Pug, there are different levels of shows that you can participate in. A good place to start would be at a "companion show" — dogs don't have to be registered with the Kennel Club, and entries are taken on the day. In addition to some classes for pedigree dogs, there will often be classes for such things as "best condition," "prettiest face," and such like. These are just for fun, but they can be good places for a novice to practice.

Following this the next step is a "limit show." Here entries are made in advance and it is confined to dogs who have not won major awards.

The "open show" is the next level and here any dogs can enter, including champions. Breeds will be scheduled and points can be achieved towards a Junior Warrant.

Photo Credit: Julia Ashton of Zobear Pugs.

The highest level is the "championship show." This is where a Cruft's qualification can be won, as well as the all-important Challenge Certificate. To be a champion, a dog needs to win three challenge certificates under three separate judges in order to achieve their title. All the males in the breed compete in their classes, and then all the winners compete against each other to win the dog CC. The same thing happens with all the bitches and then the bitch CC is awarded. The best dog and the best bitch compete against each other to produce the "best of breed."

More information can be found on the Kennel Club website, including addresses of local clubs who can help in training for shows: http://www.thekennelclub.org.uk/.

Chapter 9 — Grooming

Luckily Pugs are quite a low-maintenance dog compared to many breeds. Thanks to their short coats, Pugs stay clean, but they do shed — a lot! (single coats shed less than doubles). The more time you spend brushing your Pug, the less hair you will have on everything in the house. A good diet and grooming can keep down the shedding.

As **soon as your Pug is home,** work on desensitizing him to your touch. This will help when you come to groom him and also when you have to visit the vet's. Start slowly to begin with and build up the time as he seems comfortable. Touch areas such as his gums and nails so these areas can be maintained by you.

Photo Credit: Gail Saffer of Ragemma Pugs.

Don't allow yourself to get caught in the "my Pug doesn't like it" trap, which is an excuse many owners make to avoid regular grooming sessions. When your Pug dictates whether they will permit a grooming session, you are setting a dangerous precedent. In time, your Pug **will love** being tickled, rubbed, and scratched in certain favorite places. Grooming is a great source of pleasure and a way to bond together.

Regular brushing (**I suggest twice a week**) helps your Pug in many ways. Aerating the coat ensures healthy growth by promoting good blood circulation. It helps to keep grease levels down which can block pores and cause sebaceous cysts. He will also **shed less hair** around your house.

If you don't brush (groom) them, their loose hair becomes matted, forming heavy wads, which can cause skin complaints and soreness.

Also, toenails need to be checked every four weeks; be sure they are not hitting the floor. One can gauge this by listening to the dog walk. You should not hear the nails touching the floor; they should be "just off" the floor. This is important, as it can change the gait of the dog and eventually cause knee or hip problems.

Every week, the owner needs to trim hairs around the eyes so the corneas do not get scratched. Very importantly, clean around the eyes once a day to clean up excessive tearing and prevent tear staining.

In terms of brushes, the standard options include:

- **Bristle** brushes, which work well with all coats from long to short. They remove dirt and debris and distribute natural oils throughout the coat.

- **Wire-pin** brushes, which are for medium to long coats and look like a series of pins stuck in a raised base.

- **Slicker** brushes are excellent for smoothing and detangling longer hair.

You can often find combination, two-headed brushes. They'll save you a little money and make your grooming sessions easier.

Each of these types of brush costs less than $15 / £9 and often less than $10 / £6.

I like the ballpoint slicker brushes as the metal teeth on a normal slicker brush can be quite sharp.

Personally, I find the best grooming tool to use on your Pug at home is a wire pin brush—brush your Pug from head to toe, moving in the direction of hair growth. If you come across a mat or tangle, try to work through it with a wide-tooth comb. If you absolutely cannot get it out, you can cut it out. To do so, pinch the hair below the mat as close to your Pug's skin as you can—this will help to ensure you do not accidentally cut your dog's skin—then just cut the mat free.

Spraying the coat with a conditioner before combing will keep it shining and clean.

BREEDERS TIPS: A friend of mine swears by the **Tangle Teezer** brush. Although it's for women's hair, it apparently works like a charm. She says brushing is now fun and relaxing because her dog believes he is getting a massage.

Grooming/brushing sessions are an excellent opportunity to examine your dog's skin to do a **quick health check**. Look for any growths, lumps, bumps, or wounds. Also have a good look at his ears, eyes, and mouth. Check between paw pads for any balls of matted fur, which can become hard with dirt and grease, causing pain.

Dr. Jeff and Amy McLelland of Pickwick Pugs: "It is recommended to brush the Pug regularly to help cut down on the shedding, however we find it sufficient to only brush our Pugs after the weekly bath, for special occasions, or when getting ready for a show."

Eyes

Check your Pug's eyes daily. Usually they should be clear and bright, with no excessive discharge apart from that left over from sleeping.

Older dogs' eyes may show signs of becoming cloudy; this could be a sign of cataracts, and if you are worried, then it is worth speaking to your vet.

You should wipe their eyes regularly with a warm, damp cloth to remove the build-up of secretions in the corners of the eyes. This can be both unattractive and uncomfortable for the dog, as the hair becomes glued together. If this build-up is not removed every day, it can quickly become a cause of **bacterial yeast growth** that can lead to smelly eye infections.

Because Pugs have protruding eyes, they are more prone to eye injuries than most other dogs. If they injure an eye, rinse it with warm water and get them to the vet as soon as you can.

Heidi Merkli of Bugaboo Reg'd: "The other issue with Pugs is their eyes. As a breed prone to PK (pigment keratitis) owners should be vigilant from the start at keeping their Pug's eyes lubricated. A daily use of a tear gel will help in stalling and keeping the PK in check and reducing dry eye. Over 80% of the Pug breed can be afflicted with this issue therefore being proactive is essential to healthy eyes. A yearly visit to a veterinarian certified ophthalmologist is also a good practice to get into. Extremes in cold or dry weather, dust etc. can play a role in causing the eye to be dry not to mention the fact that Pugs do have protruding eyes as do most brachycephalic breeds. I once had an owner whose Pug got a scratch on its eye from a blade of grass; so make sure you inspect your Pug daily—as you would any pet—for overall good health."

Cleaning the Ears and Face

Your Pug's ears should be checked daily. Look for a dark discharge or regular scratching, as this can signal an infection. Affected ears have a stronger smell than usual.

Their wrinkles accumulate a great deal of dirt because Pugs spend a lot of time with their face mashed against the ground so cleaning the folds is essential to avoid them developing a fungus or infection. At least once a week, ideally daily, you should wipe the wrinkle above the nose with a damp cloth.

When grass seeds get into the ear canal they can be extremely painful and distressing for your dog. Left in they can rupture the ear drum and move into the inner ear causing serious disease. They have even been known to track all the way up legs to burst out of elbows! Look out for warning signs: sudden onset of head shaking or rubbing, holding the head at a tilt with the affected ear down, distress and/or whimpering, lameness, cysts or swellings or discharge from between the toes, or swellings around the feet.

Pugs that have a lot of hair growing inside the ear can struggle with infection, as the hair can prevent normal healthy wax leaving the ear area. Trim the hair inside the ears with safety scissors (blunted ends).

Ear mites can become a problem if your dog comes into contact with an infected animal. Too small to be seen by the naked eye, a bad ear mite infestation can cause the dog a lot of unrest and distress through itchiness. Both infections and ear mites can be diagnosed and treated easily with drops, antibiotics, or both, as prescribed by your vet.

There are many ear cleaning creams, drops, oils, rinses, solutions, and wipes formulated for cleaning ears that you can buy from your local pet store or veterinarians. You may prefer to use a home remedy that will just as efficiently clean your Pug's ears, such as **Witch Hazel** or a 50:50 mixture of hydrogen peroxide and purified water.

On a weekly basis, use a cleaner to protect your dog's ears against these potential problems. Avoid a buildup of wax, which can lead to irritation and infection, as the normal bacteria and yeasts on the skin start to multiply. Look for signs of redness down the ear, or pain, which is displayed by the Pug shaking its head. Squirt the cleaner in the ear and then fold the flap over, massaging the cleaner into the base of the ear. Allow the dog to shake its head, and then clean only the visible parts of the ear with a cotton ball. Repeat on the other side. Most ear infections are not contagious from one dog to another; you just need to take care to continue treatment as advised even if the ear looks healed.

Ear powders, which can be purchased at any pet store, are designed to help keep your Pug's ears dry while at the same time inhibiting the growth of bacteria that can lead to infections. You may want to apply a little ear powder after washing the inside of your dog's ears to help ensure that they are totally dry.

Bathing

Because the Pug has a short coat regular baths are not necessary. The cleaner the dog's environment, the less odor will be present. Using a bed stuffed with cedar or other aromatic shavings can also be a huge help, but do be cautious about allowing your dog to come into contact with anything that might trigger an allergic reaction.

Bathing a Pug too often will strip the skin of the necessary essential oils and leave the poor animal dried out and itchy. Usually Pugs only require a bath when they've gotten into something. When you do decide your pet really must have a bath, use tepid water and a good quality canine shampoo.

Christina Hedrick and Cathleen Codling of Wahoo Pugs & Pug Rescue of North Carolina, Inc: "Honestly I think any dog with fur smells more than a dog with hair. With that being said a lot plays into their diet and good grooming. A lot of dogs suffer from yeast on their skin, folds and ears, this will definitely add to a bad smelling dog. I do not smell any odor with my Pug but I bet someone that has never owned a dog might say they can smell them."

If you do need to bathe your Pug, give him a good brushing before you do. Fill your bathtub with a few inches of warm water then place your Pug in it.

Pugs can get ear infections. To prevent **your Pug's head getting wet,** clean his head and face with a warm, wet washcloth only. Rinse your dog's coat with a mixture of 1 tbsp. shampoo and 2 cups water, then pour over dog. Use clean, fresh water to remove all residue. Pugs have a dense undercoat which soaks up a lot of water so it does take considerable time to dry. Towel your pet dry and make sure he doesn't get chilled. The rinse is really the most important step of the whole procedure. If any shampoo is left in the coat, it will irritate the skin and lead to "hot spots."

TIP: Try using chamois cloths to dry your Pug. They work well, and they don't have to be laundered as much. They just air dry and can be washed in the washing machine. I have found that they work much better than towels. However, DO NOT put the chamois in the dryer.

DON'T make the mistake of using human shampoo or conditioner on your Pug, because they have a different pH balance than us and it will be too harshly acidic for their coat and skin, which can create skin problems. Purchase a shampoo **specially formulated** to be gentle and moisturizing on your Pug's coat and skin, one that will not strip the natural oils, and will nourish your dog's coat to give it a healthy shine.

Dr. Jeff and Amy McLelland of Pickwick Pugs: "Ideally, a Pug's face should be wiped off daily or bi-weekly using a baby wipe or a soft, damp cloth, particularly in the nose fold area. Pugs will also need their ears cleaned regularly, often in between baths. Pugs without a large nose fold will not need the nose cleaning beyond their weekly or bi-monthly bath."

Nail Trimming

Coat maintenance is not the only grooming chore necessary to keep your Pug in good shape. Even dogs that walk on asphalt or other rough surfaces will need to have their nails trimmed from time to time; although if you do walk your Pug a lot they won't need as much trimming. If nails get too long, they can split and get damaged more easily. Your Pug's nails are fast-growing that require a check, and most likely a cut, once a month (maybe more often).

A good time to cut their nails is **when they are fast asleep** on your lap at night. They are less likely to put up a struggle!

If your pet is agreeable, this is a job you can perform at home with a guillotine-style nail clipper especially designed for use with dogs. I prefer those with plier grips. They're easier to handle and quite cost-effective, selling for under $20 / £12.

A Dremel sanding tool can be a good alternative to clippers for trimming your dog's nails. **Never** use a regular Dremel tool, as it will be too high speed and will burn your dog's toenails. Only use a slow-speed Dremel, such as Model 7300-PT Pet Nail Grooming Tool (approx.

$40 / £28.) You can also purchase the flexible hose attachment for the Dremel, which is much easier to handle and can be held like a pencil.

Snip off the nail tips at a 45-degree angle at the point where the nail begins to curve at the tip, before the point where the pink area, referred to as the quick is (this is the nerves and blood supply that run vertically down the center of the nail). Because a Pug's nails are black it can be difficult to see the quick. If in doubt get a professional to do this.

Be careful not to cut too far down, otherwise you will hurt your Pug and cause heavy bleeding. If this happens, don't panic. Use a piece of cotton or tissue and hold pressure on it until it stops bleeding. Buy some **styptic powder** just in case. This antiseptic clotting agent causes the vessels to contract, thereby stemming the blood loss. Apply to the nail only, and a warning—initially it will sting your Pug.

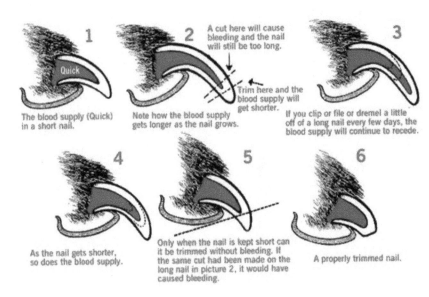

1 — The blood supply (Quick) in a short nail.

2 — A cut here will cause bleeding and the nail will still be too long. Trim here and the blood supply will get shorter. Note how the blood supply gets longer as the nail grows.

3 — If you clip or file or dremel a little off of a long nail every few days, the blood supply will continue to recede.

4 — As the nail gets shorter, so does the blood supply.

5 — Only when the nail is kept short can it be trimmed without bleeding. If the same cut had been made on the long nail in picture 2, it would have caused bleeding.

6 — A properly trimmed nail.

Dr. Jeff and Amy McLelland of Pickwick Pugs: "While brushing Pugs is straightforward, toenail trimming is the WORST. My vet offers a "free toenail trim" for my dog's birthday. I laugh every time this postcard arrives in the mail because I know what an ordeal it is for us and I would never subject my vet to this ordeal unnecessarily. I've met Pug owners who proudly state that they can do their Pug's nails with only one human, however, in our experience, it has always required two humans with exceptional wrestling skills, tremendously strong hand and arm muscles, and perhaps even a glass of wine or two as well. While my Golden Retriever/Chow mix allows me to Dremel her toenails as she calmly yet reluctantly sits on my lap, every Pug we've owned since 1990 has required one human to hold the screaming Pug and a second human to hold the Pug's foot and Dremel. The Pugs seem to tolerate the "diamond bit" on the Dremel much better. It is more expensive but worth the investment."

We asked **Vallarie Smith Cuttie of Peachtree Pugs** what common issues owners experience: "Many new Pug owners contact me after bringing their new puppy home because they are having difficulty with the pup's nail care. I show new puppy buyers how to use a sanding tool to trim the pup's nails when the puppy is picked up but a lot of people have trouble doing it themselves once they get home. It is very important to keep the pup's nails short and I recommend weekly trims while the pup is young to keep up with the rapid growth of the nails. To help new puppy owners I send them a short YouTube video showing how to wrap the pup in a towel and how to quickly but carefully grind each nail with an electric grinding tool and sandpaper drum attachment.

https://www.youtube.com/watch?v=CACNVnZAyhU

"I occasionally get a call from new puppy owners if they see their pup have an episode of reverse sneezing which is not uncommon in Pugs. I reassure them that this is nothing to be worried about and that a drop of lemon juice on the tongue usually stops the reverse sneezing."

Anal Glands

All dogs can suffer from blocked anal glands. Many dogs express them every time they poop (the sacs/glands are around a dog's anus, but occasionally the sacs fill with fluid and your Pug will need some help to release the fluid).

He may scoot or rub his bottom on the ground or carpet (you may also notice a foul odor). If this occurs, the glands will need expressing to prevent an abscess from forming. This is a sensitive task and one that a veterinarian or an experienced groomer should perform.

If your dog is fed a healthy diet this should not be a problem. My vet suggested adding a probiotic to my dog's diet when she had a problem with her anal glands at about nine years of age, and it has not reoccurred since.

Fleas and Ticks

I'm including fleas and ticks under grooming because that's when they're usually found. Don't think that if your Pug has "passengers" you're doing something wrong, or that the dog is at fault. This is a part of dog ownership. Sooner or later, it will happen. Address the problem, but don't panic.

To get rid of fleas, bathe your dog in warm water with a standard canine shampoo. I recommend you comb him at least once daily, every day during pest season with a flea comb that is fine-toothed to trap the live parasites. Submerge the comb in hot soapy water to kill the fleas. Do this on a white towel so you actually can see what's coming off your dog as you comb.

Wash the dog's bedding and any soft materials with which he has come in contact. Look for any accumulations of flea dirt, which is blood excreted by adult fleas. Wash the bedding and other surfaces daily for at least a week to kill any remaining eggs before they hatch.

While nobody likes to use chemicals on their dogs, it seems almost impossible to use anything else in the battle with fleas, ticks, and bugs! For the last decade or so, I have used a safe lawn product in my dog yards that kill fleas, ticks, spiders, mosquitoes, and more. I go by the directions and don't allow the dogs to go to those yards until after a rain or a watering after application. Since then, I usually do not need to use any other products on the dogs. I do a lawn application at the end of March, the end of June, and the last one in September.

Do NOT use a commercial flea product on a puppy of under 12 weeks of age, and be extremely careful with adult dogs. Most of the major products contain pyrethrum. The chemical can cause long-term neurological damage and even fatalities in small dogs.

TIP: Nexgard is a treatment for fleas AND also for heartworms, so it is time efficient. Also, Dawn dish soap kills fleas and is safe for all ages.

TIP: A collar, like the Seresto collar, is an innovative flea and tick collar that protects for up to eight months by a slow release of insecticide — without the need to remember monthly applications.

If your Pug is outside a lot, check for ticks on a regular basis, as these eight-legged parasites can carry diseases. Look out for warning signs such as lack of movement, swollen joints, fever, and loss of appetite.

If you find a tick, coat it with a thick layer of petroleum jelly for five minutes to suffocate the parasite and cause its jaws to release. Pluck the tick off with a pair of tweezers using a straight motion. An alternative is a tick remover, which is a tool similar to a bottle opener. Never just jerk a tick off a dog. The parasite's head stays behind and continues to burrow into the skin, making a painful sore.

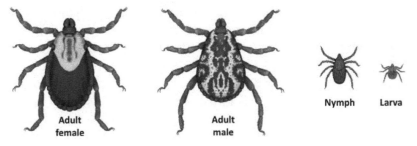
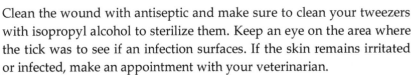

Adult
female   Adult
male   Nymph   Larva

Clean the wound with antiseptic and make sure to clean your tweezers with isopropyl alcohol to sterilize them. Keep an eye on the area where the tick was to see if an infection surfaces. If the skin remains irritated or infected, make an appointment with your veterinarian.

Many breeders are choosing to avoid harsh chemicals and over-vaccination, and instead are using homeopathic nosodes and natural wormers, as well as working on keeping their dogs' immune systems healthy. They tend to feed them a raw, species-appropriate diet and don't treat their dogs for fleas unless they see them.

They also do regular worm counts on their older dogs to see if they actually have worms. **Diotomaceous earth** added to the food daily helps to keep your dog clear of worms but if you purchase it make sure it's food grade. For dogs that don't like extras added to their food, I use **Four Seasons**. Ground pumpkin seeds can also be used.

TIP: For a natural organic spray that repels ticks and fleas, try Herbal Defense Spray by PetzLife. Ruff on Bugs is a similar spray consisting of essential oils such as lemongrass, cinnamon, cedar, citronella, geranium, and rosemary, in non-GMO oils.

Home Dental Care

Pugs don't have great teeth due to the shape of their jaws. You will need to look out for bad breath, tartar build-up and gingivitis. Fortunately there are many products available to help with home dental care for your Pug. Some owners opt for water additives that break up tartar and plaque, but in some cases dogs experience stomach upset. Dental sprays and wipes are also an option, but so is gentle gum massage to help break up plaque and tartar.

Most owners incorporate some type of dental chew in their standard care practices. Greenies Dental Chews for Dogs are popular and well tolerated in a digestive sense. An added plus is that dogs usually love them. The treats come in different sizes and are priced in a range of about $7 / £4.50 for 22 "Teeny Greenies" and $25 / £15 for 17 "Large Greenies."

Indigenous Dental Health Bones are safe and highly digestible for all dog breeds and sizes. They are made with ascophyllum nodosum, a natural kelp harvested from the clean, cold North Atlantic seas of Canada, Iceland, and Norway. This kelp is a rich source of nutrients and is free from artificial colors and preservatives.

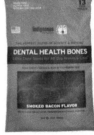

The Pug's bottom jaw is slightly longer that the top jaw (this is known as undershot) causing the teeth to be differently positioned compared with other breeds.

Your Pug should have forty-two permanent teeth. At the front are six incisors in each jaw, which cut food. Next are the canines (two in each jaw), and these tear and hold food, and then the premolars (eight in each jaw) for cutting and tearing. At the very back of the mouth are the molars used for grinding—four on the top and six on the bottom.

Brushing your pet's teeth is the ultimate defense for oral health. This involves the use of both a canine-specific toothbrush and toothpaste. Never use human toothpaste, which contains fluoride, which is toxic to your dog. Some dog toothbrushes resemble smaller versions of our own, but I like the models that just fit over your fingertip. I think they offer greater control and stability.

The real trick to brushing your pet's teeth is getting the dog comfortable with having your hands in his mouth. Start by just massaging the dog's face, and then progressing to the gums before using the toothbrush. In the beginning, you can even just smear the toothpaste on the teeth with your fingertip.

Schedule these brushing sessions for when the dog is a little tired, perhaps after a long walk. Don't apply pressure, which can stress him. Just move in small circular motions and stop when the Pug has had enough of the whole business. Even, if you don't feel you've done enough, stop. A second session is better than forcing your dog to do something he doesn't like and creating a negative association in his mind.

Even if you do practice a full home dental care routine, don't scrimp on annual oral examinations in the vet's office because the Pug often needs additional treatment, which will be performed under general anesthetic. Exams not only help to keep the teeth and gums healthy, but also to check for the presence of possible cancerous growths.

TIP: If your dog will not let you brush their teeth, allow him to chew on knuckle bones, bull pizzles, cow ears, or trachea. These all help remove tartar and stimulate the gums.

TIP: Dog breath is best tackled with the dog chewing on a raw meaty bone. If that doesn't suit, try raw fibrous vegetables (whole carrots, cabbage cores, broccoli stalks, etc.) or dried fish skin.

Chapter 10 — Training and Problem Behaviors

Pugs are really delightful companion animals. They're fun. They love to play, and they'll resort to almost any gag to make sure your attention is firmly on them. But, Pugs also know how to "work" their humans. If a Pug is badly spoiled, like any dog, he can become a little tyrant. Any dog, regardless of breed can exhibit poor behaviors.

Negative behavior may not target humans. Just because Pugs are little, don't think they won't show the kind of aggression present in any breed. In fact, it's often the little dogs that are the worst when it comes to snapping, lunging, pushing, barking, or baring of the teeth. Thankfully, Pugs are generally quite good with all types of animals, but they need socialization, just like any dog, especially if there are no other pets in the household.

Photo Credit: Wendy Davenschot of Viking Mops, Pugtography.

Michelle Chisholm of Siosalach Pugs: "I believe that Pugs can be stubborn and this can cause a challenge in training. However they have an eagerness to please and their love of food are huge assets in training. They can be great obedience dogs and rally obedience and agility dogs with consistent and positive motivation training."

It is to your advantage to go through a basic obedience class with your dog. All dogs respond well to a consistent routine and to a command "language." Provide both of these vital foundations to have a well-behaved pet.

Experts agree that most dogs can pick up between 165 and 200 words, but they can't extrapolate more than one meaning. If, for instance, your dog barks, you need to use the same command in response, like "quiet." If he picks something up, you might say "drop it."

For problem jumping, most owners go with "off" or "down." The point is to pick a set of words and use them over and over to create a basic vocabulary for your dog. Both the word and your tone of voice should convey your authority and elicit the desired response.

Pugs have a tremendous amount of energy that can be negatively expressed when they are bored or suffering from anxiety. Aggression toward other dogs is usually triggered by the Pug's territorial urge to protect his "possessions" — his crate, his food bowl, his house, and you.

Understanding their mentality is key to living successfully with this breed. At that point when their native intelligence runs smack into their obstinacy, you can have a little tyrant on your hands. Knowing how your Pug's mind works will help with training. The fact is they are super smart dogs that have a 'what's in it for me' attitude to learning new behaviors. They are also very playful. So we train based on rewards and fun to get an obedient Pug.

Pugs are good watch dogs. They will alert you to the presence of strangers, but will then warm up quickly when they see you're okay with the visitor. If you do get involved in a situation where your dog is the one acting out toward another animal with any of the typical threat displays like snapping, lunging, pushing, barking, or baring its teeth, you need to be the one who takes charge.

When it comes to dog training, there are several different methods to choose from. For Pugs, however, positive reinforcement training is the most effective. With this type of training you reward your dog for performing desired behaviors and, in doing so, reinforce that behavior.

If your dog gets a treat for sitting when you tell him to sit, he will be more likely to repeat that behavior in the future.

Pugs have an eager-to-please attitude that will help to speed up the process. The key to training your Pug effectively is to make things as simple as possible and to make sure that your dog understands what you want him to do. If you do not consistently reward your Pug for performing the desired behavior during the early stages of training, he may not learn which behavior it is that you want or he might become frustrated.

Previously, I discussed leash training, which is crucial for successful public outings. Rather than avoiding areas with other people and dogs, your goal is to be able to take your dog to such places without incident.

Pugs thrive on interaction with their humans and can be happily engaged in interesting public places like parks, walking trails, or beaches that are full of new sights, sounds, and smells. Contrary to what some people think, well-managed outings in varied environments help to create confidence in your dog.

A Pug will "shut down" with any harsh correction, so having a fun and positive training session is a must—as well as very good treats (mine like liver or chicken)!

Keep training sessions short and fun, and end with a game or a special toy. It is OK to be silly with a Pug—they enjoy it! A high pitch to your voice and lots of love is appreciated. I say '"YES" when they do something right and give an immediate treat.

If you do use a leash, try using a separate leash for training and they will learn to tell the difference between this and a regular walking leash. Most of all, you will need patience and a sense of humor to train a Pug.

Responsible dog owners are attentive to the behavior of their own dog and to what's going on around them. They praise good behavior, but accept responsibility for anticipating potential clashes.

Obedience training is essential to have a well-behaved Pug that will respond to your commands regardless of the situation. A training class exposes your puppy to new sights, sounds, people, and places. There he can interact with other dogs in a controlled environment and deal safely with any feelings of fear and timidity or territoriality and dominance. The time and effort are well worth it to get a better-mannered dog and a greater understanding of how to guide your pet's future interactions.

Dog Whispering

Many people can be confused when they need professional help with their dog because for many years, if you needed help with your dog, you contacted a "dog trainer", or took your dog to "puppy classes," where your dog would learn how to sit or stay.

The difference between a dog trainer and a dog whisperer is that a dog trainer teaches a dog how to perform certain tasks, and a dog whisperer alleviates behavior problems by teaching humans what they need to do to keep their particular dog happy.

Often, depending on how soon the guardian has sought help, this can mean that the dog in question has developed some pretty serious issues, such as aggressive barking, lunging, biting, or attacking other dogs, pets, or people.

Dog whispering is often an emotional roller coaster ride for the humans involved that unveils many truths when they finally realize that it has been their actions (or inactions) that have likely caused the unbalanced behavior that their dog is now displaying. Once solutions are provided, the relief for both dog and human can be quite cathartic when they realize that with the correct direction, they can indeed live a happy life with their dog.

All specific methods of training, such as "clicker" training, fall outside of what every dog needs to be happy, because training your dog to respond to a clicker, which you can easily do on your own, and then letting them sleep in your bed, eat from your plate, and any other multitude of things humans allow, are what makes the dog unbalanced and causes behavior problems.

I always say to people, don't wait until you have a severe problem before getting some dog whispering or professional help of some sort, because with the proper training, Man can learn to be dog's best friend.

Don't Reward Bad Behavior

It is very important to recognize that any attention paid to an out-of-control, adolescent puppy, even negative attention, is likely to be exciting and rewarding for your Pug puppy.

Photo Credit: Julia Ashton of Zobear Pugs.

Chasing after a puppy when they have taken something they shouldn't have, picking them up when barking or showing aggression, pushing them off when they jump on other people, or yelling when they refuse to come when called are all forms of attention that can actually be rewarding for most puppies.

It will be your responsibility to provide structure for your puppy, which will include finding acceptable and safe ways to allow your puppy to vent his energy without being destructive or harmful to others.

The worst thing you can do when training your Pug is to yell at him or use punishment. Positive reinforcement training methods—that is, rewarding your dog for good behavior—are infinitely more effective than negative reinforcement—training by punishment.

It is important when training your Pug that you do not allow yourself to get frustrated. If you feel yourself starting to get angry, take a break and come back to the training session later. Why is punishment-based training so bad? Think about it this way—your dog should listen to you because he wants to please you, right?

If you train your dog using punishment, he could become fearful of you and that could put a damper on your relationship with him. Do your dog and yourself a favor by using positive reinforcement.

Teaching Basic Commands

When it comes to training your Pug, you have to start off slowly with the basic commands. The most popular basic commands for dogs include sit, down, stay, and come.

Sit

This is the most basic and one of the most important commands you can teach your Pug.

1. Stand in front of your Pug with a few small treats in your pocket.

2. Hold one treat in your dominant hand and wave it in front of your Pug's nose so he gets the scent.

3. Give the "Sit" command.

4. Move the treat upward and backward over your Pug's head so he is forced to raise his head to follow it.

5. In the process, his bottom will lower to the ground.

6. As soon as your Pug's bottom hits the ground, praise him and give him the treat.

7. Repeat this process several times until your dog gets the hang of it and responds consistently.

Down

After the "Sit" command, "Down" is the next logical command to teach because it is a progression from "Sit."

1. Kneel in front of your Pug with a few small treats in your pocket.

2. Hold one treat in your dominant hand and give your Pug the "Sit" command.

3. Reward your Pug for sitting, and then give him the "Down" command.

4. Quickly move the treat down to the floor between your Pug's paws.

5. Your dog will follow the treat and should lie down to retrieve it.

6. Praise and reward your Pug when he lies down.

7. Repeat this process several times until your dog gets the hang of it and responds consistently.

Come

It is very important that your Pug responds to a "Come" command, because there may come a time when you need to get his attention and call him to your side during a dangerous situation (such as him running around too close to traffic).

1. Put your Pug on a short leash and stand in front of him.

2. Give your Pug the "Come" command, then quickly take a few steps backward away from him.

3. Clap your hands and act excited, but do not repeat the "Come" command.

4. Keep moving backwards in small steps until your Pug follows and comes to you.

5. Praise and reward your Pug and repeat the process.

6. Over time, you can use a longer leash or take your Pug off the leash entirely.

7. You can also start by standing further from your Pug when you give the "Come" command.

8. If your Pug doesn't come to you immediately, you can use the leash to pull him toward you.

Stay

This command is very important because it teaches your Pug discipline—not only does it teach your Pug to stay, but it also forces him to listen and pay attention to you.

1. Find a friend to help you with this training session.

2. Have your friend hold your Pug on the leash while you stand in front of the dog.

3. Give your Pug the "Sit" command and reward him for responding correctly.

4. Give your dog the "Stay" command while holding your hand out like a "Stop" sign.

5. Take a few steps backward away from your dog and pause for one or two seconds.

6. Step back toward your Pug, then praise and reward your dog.

7. Repeat the process several times, and then start moving back a little farther before you return to your dog.

Beyond Basic Training

Once your Pug has a firm grasp on the basics, you can move on to teaching him additional commands. You can also add distractions to the equation to reinforce your dog's mastery of the commands.

The end goal is to ensure that your Pug responds to your command each and every time—regardless of distractions and anything else he might rather be doing. This is incredibly important, because there may come a time when your dog is in a dangerous situation and if he doesn't respond to your command, he could get hurt.

Photo Credit: Julie Squire & Holly Attwood of Taftazini.

If you previously conducted your training sessions indoors, you might consider moving them outside where your dog could be distracted by various sights, smells, and sounds.

One thing you might try is to give your dog the Stay command and then toss a toy nearby that will tempt him to break his Stay. Start by tossing the toy at a good distance from him and wait a few seconds before you release him to play. Eventually you will be able to toss a toy right next to your dog without him breaking his Stay until you give him permission to do so.

Incorporating Hand Signals

Teaching your Pug to respond to hand signals in addition to verbal commands is very useful—you never know when you will be in a situation where your dog might not be able to hear you.

To start out, choose your dominant hand to give the hand signals, and hold a small treat in that hand while you are training your dog — this will encourage your dog to focus on your hand during training, and it will help to cement the connection between the command and the hand signal.

Give your dog the Sit or Down command and give the appropriate hand signal — for Sit, you might try a closed fist and for Down, you might place your hand flat, parallel to the ground.

When your dog responds correctly, give him the treat. You will need to repeat this process many times in order for your dog to form a connection between both the verbal command and the hand signal with the desired behavior.

Eventually, you can start to remove the verbal command from the equation—use the hand gesture every time, but start to use the verbal command only half the time.

Once your dog gets the hang of this, you should start to remove the food reward from the equation. Continue to give your dog the hand signal for each command, and occasionally use the verbal command just to remind him.

Teaching Distance Commands

In addition to getting your dog to respond to hand signals, it is also useful to teach him to respond to your commands even when you are not directly next to him.

This may come in handy if your dog is running around outside and gets too close to the street—you should be able to give him a Sit or Down command so he stops before he gets into a dangerous situation. Teaching your dog distance commands is not difficult, but it does require some time and patience.

To start, give your Pug a brief refresher course of the basic commands while you are standing or kneeling right next to him.

Next, give your dog the Sit and Stay commands, then move a few feet away before you give the Come command.

Repeat this process, increasing the distance between you and your dog before giving him the Come command. Be sure to praise and reward your dog for responding appropriately when he does so.

Once your dog gets the hang of coming from a distance on command, you can start to incorporate other commands. One method of doing so is to teach your dog to sit when you grab his collar. To do so, let your dog wander freely and every once in a while, walk up and grab his collar while giving the Sit command.

After a few repetitions, your dog should begin to respond with a Sit when you grab his collar, even if you do not give the command. Gradually, you can increase the distance from which you come to grab his collar and give him the command.

After your dog starts to respond consistently when you come from a distance to grab his collar, you can start giving the Sit command without moving toward him. It may take your dog a few times to get the hang of it, so be patient. If your dog doesn't sit right away, calmly walk up to him and repeat the Sit command, but do not grab his collar this time.

Eventually, your dog will get the hang of it, and you can start to practice using other commands like Down and Stay from a distance.

Clicker Training

To help speed up the training process for your Pug, you might want to look into clicker training. Clicker training is a version of positive reinforcement training.

When it comes to training your Pug, you are going to be most successful if you maintain consistency. Unless you are very clear with your dog about what your expectations are, he may simply decide not to follow your commands.

A simple way to achieve consistency in training your Pug is to use the principles of clicker training. This involves using a small handheld device that makes a clicking noise when you press it between your fingers.

Clicker training is based on the theory of operant conditioning, which helps your dog to make the connection between the desired behavior and the offering of a reward.

Photo Credit: Lundi Blamey of Claripugs.

Pugs have a natural desire to please, so if they learn that a certain behavior earns your approval, they will be eager to repeat it—this is a great way to help your dog quickly identify the particular behavior you want him to repeat.

All you have to do is give your Pug a command and, as soon as he performs the behavior, you use the clicker. After you use the clicker, give your dog the reward as you would with any form of positive reinforcement training. You should only use the clicker for the first few times to make sure that your Pug doesn't become dependent on the sound to perform the behavior.

Use food rewards during the early stages of training for positive reinforcement, but phase them out after your Pug gets the hang of each command.

Some of the benefits of clicker training include:

• Very easy to implement—all you need is the clicker.

• Helps your dog form a connection between the command and the desired behavior more quickly.

• You only need to use the clicker until your dog makes the connection then you can stop.

• May help to keep your dog's attention more effectively if he hears the noise.

Clicker training is just one method of positive reinforcement training that you can consider for training your Pug. No matter what method you choose, it is important that you maintain consistency and always praise and reward your dog for responding to your command correctly so he learns to repeat the behavior.

First Tricks

When teaching your Pug his first tricks, in order to give him extra incentive, find a small treat that he would do anything to get, and give the treat as a reward to help solidify a good performance.

Most dogs will be extra attentive during training sessions when they know that they will be rewarded with their favorite treats.

If your Pug is less than six months old when you begin teaching him tricks, keep your training sessions short (no more than five or ten minutes) and make the sessions lots of fun. As your Pug becomes an adult, you can extend your sessions because he will be able to maintain his focus for longer periods of time.

Playing Dead

Once your Pug knows the command to lie down, which should be one of the basic obedience commands he learns at "school," getting him to "play dead" is simple.

Once the dog is lying down, hold a treat in front of your pet close enough for him to smell it. Move the treat in circles toward the floor giving your Pug the command, "Play Dead."

The motion should encourage the dog to roll over on his back. As soon as he achieves the correct position, praise him and give him the treat

Pugs love treats so much, it won't take your pet long to put it all together and execute the maneuver on command.

Shake a Paw

Who doesn't love a dog who knows how to shake a paw? This is one of the easiest tricks to teach your Pug.

Practice every day until he is 100% reliable with this trick, and then it will be time to add another trick to their repertoire.

Most dogs are naturally either right- or left-pawed. If you know which paw your dog favors, ask him to shake this paw.

Find a quiet place to practice, without noisy distractions or other pets, and stand or sit in front of your dog. Place him in the sitting position and hold a treat in your left hand.

Say the command "Shake" while putting your right hand behind his left or right paw and pulling the paw gently toward yourself until you are holding his paw in your hand. Immediately praise him and give them the treat.

Most dogs will learn the "Shake" trick very quickly, and in no time at all, once you put out your hand, your Pug will immediately lift his paw and put it into your hand without your assistance or any verbal cue.

Give Me Five

The next trick after "Shake" should be "High Five." Teach this sequence the same way, but when you hold out your hand to shake, move your hand up and touch your dog's paw saying, "High Five!" It may take a few tries, but by this time your Pug will be getting the idea that if he learns his lessons, he gets his treat.

This set of four tricks is a good example of using one behavior to build up to another. Almost any dog can be taught to perform basic tricks, but don't lose sight of the fact that you are dealing with an individual personality. You may have a Pug that would rather chase his chew toys than learn "routines." Get to know what your dog enjoys doing and follow his lead to build his unique set of tricks.

Roll Over

You will find that just like your Pug is naturally either right or left-pawed, that he will also naturally want to roll to either the right or the left side.

Take advantage of this by asking your dog to roll to the side he naturally prefers. Sit with your dog on the floor and put him in a lying-down position.

Hold a treat in your hand and place it close to his nose without allowing him to grab it, and while he is in the lying position, move the treat to the right or left side of the head so that he has to roll over to get to it.

You will quickly see which side he wants to naturally roll to; once you see this, move the treat to that side. Once he rolls over to that side, immediately give him the treat and praise him.

You can say the verbal cue "Over" while you demonstrate the hand signal motion (moving your right hand in a half circular motion) from one side of their head to the other.

Sit Pretty

While this trick is a little more complicated, most dogs pick up on it very quickly, but remember that this trick requires balance, and every dog is different, so always exercise patience.

Find a quiet space with few distractions and sit or stand in front of your dog and ask him to "Sit."

Have a treat nearby (on a countertop or table) and when they sit, use both of your hands to lift up their front paws into the sitting pretty position, while saying the command "Sit Pretty." Help them balance in this position while you praise them and give them the treat.

Once your Pug can do the balancing part of the trick quite easily without your help, sit or stand in front of your dog while asking him to "Sit Pretty" and hold the treat above their head, at the level their nose would be when he "sits pretty."

If they attempt to stand on their back legs to get the treat, you may be holding the treat too high, which will encourage them to stand up on their back legs to reach it. Go back to the first step and put them back into the "Sit" position, and again lift their paws while their backside remains on the floor.

The hand signal for "Sit Pretty" is a straight arm held over your dog's head with a closed fist. Place your Pug beside a wall when first teaching this trick so that they can use the wall to help their balance.

A young Pug puppy should be able to easily learn these basic tricks before they are six months old, and when you are patient and make your training sessions short and fun for your dog, they will be eager to learn more.

Photo Credit: Michelle Chisholm of Siosalach Pugs.

Excessive Jumping

Allowing any dog to jump is a serious mistake. It is one of the most undesirable of all traits in a companion canine. Many people are afraid of dogs and find spontaneous jumping threatening. Since Pugs are prone to hip dysplasia and luxating patella, allowing your dog to jump is an invitation for pain for him and high vet bills for you.

If you do have a dog that is bored and suffering from anxiety, his hyperactivity will kick in and he may begin to jump up on people.

Don't assume that excessive jumping is an expression of friendliness. All too often it's a case of a dominant dog asserting his authority and saying, "I don't respect you." Dogs that know their proper place in the "pack" don't jump on more dominant dogs—or on more dominant humans! A jumper sees himself as the "top dog" in all situations.

As the dog's master, you must enforce the "no jumping" rule. Anything else will only confuse your pet. Dogs have a keen perception of space. Rather than retreating from a jumping dog, step sideways and forward, taking back your space that he is trying to claim.

You are not trying to knock your dog down, but he may career into you and fall anyway. Remain casual and calm. Take slow, deliberate motions and protect the "bubble" around your body. Your dog won't be expecting this action from you, and won't enjoy it.

After several failed jumps the dog will lose interest when his dominant message is no longer getting across.

It is important to praise him when he does have all four feet on the ground. Rewarding good behavior is often forgotten.

TIPS FROM EXPERT BREEDERS: Let's begin by saying that you have to establish right away who the pack leader is. This is KEY in all aspects of owning an obedient, respectful dog. Please keep in mind that dogs understand dog language. If a momma dog has an issue with her young, she would never tolerate it. If she sees something she doesn't like, she will move the puppy in a calm assertive manner, out of the way. She uses her body to teach boundaries. You can use yours too. When you have a dog that habitually jumps up, he or she is establishing that they are your pack leader. Gain control of this by teaching your dog simple commands. This is imperative to having a great, social member of society. When you come in and you are greeted by your dog, make him sit before being petted. If he jumps on you, gently meet him or her with a raised knee, a firm "OFF" and follow with the command "SIT." Praise your dog when you get the desired results. You must be consistent! Remember, you also must establish from the beginning (puppy stage) that you are the pack leader. A pack leader never negotiates. If you are inconsistent it could lead to role reversal, creating a dog that is confused, nervous, anxious, and one that may never be house-trainable. Think like a dog and you will be very successful at being TOP DOG!

Barking Behavior

Excessive barking creates serious problems, especially if you live near other people. Normally Pugs will bark a few times in greeting and then quieten down, but if they don't like something, or they are allowed to get in the habit of barking, a Pug can be just as relentless with his voice as any breed.

A Pug's bark can be highly amusing. Their voices are rather high-pitched, and they tend to snuffle and dance around while they're barking. If a Pug thinks something he's doing is pleasing you, he'll do it over and over again. No matter how funny you may think your dog's bark is, don't encourage him to become a barker by laughing at him!

If you are in an apartment complex with shared walls, a barking dog can get you thrown out of your home. The answer to problem barking in Pugs is usually more exercise and intellectual stimulation, but if these simple solutions don't work, you may need the help of an expert to figure out what is setting your dog off.

Your Pug may bark for the following reasons:

Boredom — Being left alone for long periods of time causes sadness.

Fear — They may sense a threat such as another animal.

Greeting — They love to greet visitors, or perhaps on a walk they want to communicate with another dog. This would usually be accompanied with a wagging tail and maybe jumping up.

Getting Attention — He may need to go outside to go to the toilet, or maybe he wants attention from you or food.

So, what can you do when you have an issue?

1. Nip it in the bud by dealing with barking problems as quickly as possible before it escalates.

2. Fence your garden or yard with solid fencing so he feels safer and less threatened.

3. Ignore your Pug until he stops barking. You don't want him thinking he can just bark and get what he wants, or he will only keep repeating the behavior.

4. If he barks while you're out and the neighbors complain, he is bored. Don't leave him as long; get someone to come in and play with him or leave toys that occupy him.

5. As with all problem behaviors, address barking with patience and consistency. Don't shout and get angry—he will bark even louder.

6. You can feed him a treat AFTER as a reward but never when he is barking, otherwise he will start to bark to get a treat!

7. For real problem barkers, humane bark collars can teach the dog through negative reinforcement. These collars release a harmless spray of citronella into the dog's nose in response to vibrations in the throat. The system, though somewhat expensive at around $100 / £60, works in almost all cases.

TIPS FROM EXPERT BREEDERS: Barking is a natural way of communication for our pets. It is important that you are always the pack leader. Every habit picked up by dogs can be easily corrected if you maintain this status early on. It is the language that dogs can understand and relate to. A lot of times, excess barking is a result of pent-up or excess energy. Take lots of time to interact with your dog and the problems that arise from a frustrated dog will be fewer. When a dog is barking, divert their attention. Hopefully you have been consistent in your interaction with your dog and you have established some simple commands. If you haven't, this is a good place to start.

Teach sit, down, stay, off, and come/recall. Once you have these commands successfully instilled in your dog, the command "QUIET" will be a lot easier. The use of a leash if your dog is outside or inside is very helpful. You can grab the leash and divert his or her attention while they are barking by grabbing the leash and redirecting their attention to you with a command of "NO BARK" or "Quiet," whichever you prefer. I can't stress enough how consistency is key, along with having already established your alpha status. If you are unsuccessful at teaching these commands, please seek the advice of a professional.

The personality of the dog determines the amount of barking, potentially. Other puppies in that same litter may not be so prone to bark. Often enough, in a litter the 'loud-mouth' is the dominant dog. Is this nature's way of the dog protecting his pack?

The next time your dog starts barking, see if there is definite stimulus and if not, try spending time with the dog. My barkers tend to bark when there are other strange dogs near 'their' fence or when I am working with another of my dogs. Most Pugs will bark when the owner comes home, but this is a happy bark and should stop as soon as you give the dogs a hello cuddle.

Chasing

Pugs like to play and chase toys, and will want to chase things during outings. This is behavior you want to discourage not only for obvious safety reasons, but also because Pugs are a **heat-intolerant breed**, another consequence of being brachycephalic.

When you are out with your Pug dog, especially in busy urban areas, you must keep your pet leashed at all times. Never allow your dog off the leash unless you are in a fenced, completely secure area. Pay close attention to the temperature and make sure your Pug has access to shade and water.

Puppies love to play chase and often the human animal is the one doing the chasing. Start with young puppies and teach them that when they run away, **you do not chase**. Instead, turn and walk a few paces away, squat or sit down and **IGNORE** the puppy. The puppy will usually come to you to play. Let the puppy touch you and then you scratch, pat, and cuddle the puppy. Giving a treat at this time will also help teach the puppy not to run away. Gradually, as the puppy grows, start using 'come' to begin teaching this command.

Chewing

Chewing is a natural behavior in dogs and is a recognized disobedience issue with Pugs. If left undirected, a dog with a fetish for chewing is capable of causing unbelievable levels of destruction in your home. Excessive chewing indicates some combination of anxiety or boredom, which may mean you need to get your dog out of the house more.

Normal chewing relieves anxiety, keeps their jaws strong and their teeth clean. However, excessive chewing needs to be curbed. Make sure you are giving your Pug plenty of physical and mental stimulation by taking him to the dog park, playing games such as fetch, or enrolling him in activities such as agility training.

Puppies go through a teething stage like human babies, when they lose their baby teeth and experience pain as their adult teeth grow through. This should be done with by about twelve months, but before that you can still channel your puppy's urge to chew in the right direction. Make sure your dog has proper chew toys that exist to be destroyed! Keep things interesting by buying new ones every so often.

Yes, you can give him a bone, but only natural bones that are sold specifically for chewing, because cooked bones can splinter and seriously injure him.

If you catch your pet chewing on a forbidden object, reprimand (I don't mean punish) him and take the item away. Immediately substitute an appropriate chew toy and if you choose to, reward him with attention or a treat.

Photo Credit: Christina Givens of Wind Valley Pugs.

Never give a puppy a shoe to chew on—he will always think shoes are to chew on and will not know the difference between the cheap shoes and expensive shoes. All puppies will chew, and just like human babies—teething means chewing.

I give a teething puppy carrot batons to chew into; they're cool and soothing on the gums. I also give my adult Pugs carrots as treats, which of course, they love!

You can buy chewing deterrents such as Grannick's Bitter Apple spray, which you spray on all objects that you don't want your dog to chew. Reapply the deterrent every day for two to four weeks.

TIPS FROM EXPERT BREEDERS: We have to be mindful of the fact that from three to eight weeks old, puppies are getting their deciduous teeth. Those teeth will then be replaced by their permanent teeth from four to six months. These are the times that chewing is at its most painful. Their gums are very irritated, and chewing is their natural instinct at this time. This can lead to a long-standing problem, however, if you do not get it under control. Please always rule out any potential medical problem that may be causing the excess chewing. Always maintain alpha dog status. This will help with them chewing your belongings. Puppy proof your home. Do not let puppy have free access to your home, and never unsupervised.

Provide acceptable chew items, like raw bones, antlers, and perhaps a Kong with organic peanut butter in it. Never feed cooked bones or rawhide, and always supervise your dog when he has something to chew on. Deter your dog from chewing on unacceptable items with a replacement of acceptable things. Dogs benefit greatly from exercise. A dog that is stimulated by exercise is usually one that will rest when playtime or walk time is over.

If you find your puppy chewing on something he shouldn't, say 'give' and take it away from him gently. Always give your puppy the proper chew toy in trade, telling him 'take' and then 'good boy' after he has the 'right' toy in his mouth. If he resists giving you the 'bad' toy, slowly put pressure at the back of the jaw where the upper and lower teeth meet. Make sure you press with the skin of the cheek between your fingers and his teeth. That way if he bites down he is actually hurting himself. Remember to give the command 'give' and praise him after he has taken the trade toy.

Digging

Digging, like other problem behaviors, is an expression of fear, anxiety, and/or boredom and something a Pug can do with ruthless efficiency!

Digging is a difficult behavior to stop with any breed. An out-of-control digger in the house can destroy your sofa or some other piece of furniture. If you cannot be home during the day to give your Pug the interaction he craves, enroll your pet in a dog daycare facility. He'll love going to "work" every day and you'll be saved walking into a wrecked house.

Most diggers do so for specific reasons. Again, try thinking like a dog. Is your dog digging to make a cool bed, chasing a bug, burying a toy, or because of boredom? You cannot put a puppy or dog into the backyard and not spend quality time with them. They will find ways to entertain themselves and your freshly planted flower garden (your smell will be strongest there) will be just too tempting! Also, some dogs will dig to get out. Dogs will get bored and they are by instinct pack animals. If there are other dogs to go play with and your dog does not get enough attention from YOU, then he will seek out other pack members.

Begging

If there is any one major Pug "problem" I would point to after the difficulty of housebreaking, I'd have to put begging at the top of the list. Cliché or not, it's perfectly accurate to call a Pug a chow hound. They love their groceries, and they are superior beggars, armed with those big dark eyes, those expressive wrinkles, and that devastating ability to cock their heads to the side at just the right moment.

Don't be at all surprised if you walk in the kitchen to find your Pug on the counter. The dining room table is no stretch for his abilities. Never leave food within a Pug's reach or it will be gone.

Do not let this get started! Obesity is a major and life-threatening problem with this breed. Any dog will beg at the table if allowed to do so, but Pugs are among the worst canine panhandlers on the planet. Make "people" food off limits from day one and stick to your guns.

If your pet becomes a serious beggar, confine him to another part of the house during meal times. Pugs want so much to be with their people, that being put somewhere else during meals may be all that's needed to convince them to turn down the "starving to death" routine at which they excel. If you can't ignore a set of pleading Pug eyes imploring you to share your dinner, you're the real problem!

Biting

Pugs are not known to be problem biters, but any dog will bite if he is reacting out of pain or fear. Biting is a primary means of defense. Use socialization, obedience training, and stern corrections to control a puppy's playful nips.

With their littermates, your Pug would have learned about bite inhibition, which is a dog's ability to control the pressure he uses when biting so that he doesn't cause pain or harm. When puppies are playing, if they bite too hard the other puppy will yelp or run away, which teaches the puppy not to bite so hard. This would have curbed the rough play, and this technique can be used when this nipping becomes painful or dangerous to you.

If your Pug puppy has a tendency to bite you a little harder than you think he should, you can teach him bite inhibition yourself. When playing with your puppy if he bites you, you should say "Ouch!" in a calm tone and gently remove your hand from his mouth to imitate the reaction, as if from a sibling in the pack. After you do, stop paying attention to the puppy for a few seconds before resuming play. It may also be helpful for you to give your puppy a chew toy after removing your hand, so he learns what he is and is not allowed to chew on.

Obviously, any dog will bite if he is reacting out of pain or fear. However, if an adult dog displays biting behavior, it is imperative to get to the bottom of the biting. Have the dog evaluated for a health problem and work with a professional trainer.

TIPS FROM EXPERT BREEDERS: Never allow or encourage children to hit the puppy. The puppy will naturally want to 'catch' the moving hand, and a future biter may be in the beginning stages. The same goes for a puppy that chases and bites. Do not run from the puppy; stop, tell him no and then ignore him. Running from the puppy is fun to the puppy. You can teach the puppy to follow by walking calmly, calling his name, and giving a treat. When giving a puppy a treat, always say 'easy' and never jerk the food away. Encourage your puppy to take food from your hand from the beginning. Hopefully, the breeder has already started hand-feeding treats at weaning.

Dealing with Copraphagia

Copraphagia is when dogs eat feces, either their own or that of another animal. While we may be appalled at this, it is actually quite common in dogs. The problem is that nobody really seems to know why this happens. Reasons speculated upon include a lack of nutrition in their diet, being left alone, or learned behavior from their time in the litter.

Mostly they will grow out of this, but how can we discourage it?

1. Clean up after him as soon as he has eliminated.

2. Keep him stimulated with chew toys and games and don't leave him alone for long periods.

3. Review his diet — Vitamin-B deficiency is a key suspect, but it could be another nutrient he is lacking.

You could feed certain foods that are expelled and smell disgusting to him, so he avoids eating them. These include parsley and courgettes/zucchinis.

I have also had puppies start this habit as soon as they were started on commercial dog food. Check with your veterinarian for his or her suggestions. There are numerous commercial products that might help curb or stop this problem.

Chapter 11 — Pug Health

You are your Pug's primary healthcare provider. You will know what is "normal" for your dog. Yours will be the best sense that something is "wrong" even when there is no obvious injury or illness. The more you understand preventive healthcare, the better you will care for your Pug throughout his life.

There isn't any breed of dog without a genetic weakness and most breeds have not just one, but several ailments that they are more likely to inherit than other breeds. The genetic abnormalities and illnesses that surface most in the Pug are often related to their brachycephalic features and compact build. These problems include ocular, respiratory, and orthopedic conditions among others.

We asked **Judith Johnson of Foursquare Pugs** about the most common health issues seen in Pugs: "My husband David is a veterinarian and the most reasons Pugs are seen in his practice, aside from routine exams and vaccines, are eye problems, overweight and overheating. These are the same problems that I feel new owners need to know about Pugs. When we send a puppy to a new home we also send along a booklet explaining some of the health issues they might encounter with their Pugs. This includes a section on eyes, a section on the correct feeding of a Pug, a page on PDE and a section on hot and cold weather husbandry."

Julianne McCoy of Low Country Pugs: "The health of Pugs in the United States has improved in the last five to ten years. We now test for PDE (Pug Dog Encephalitis). We also are required to do many other tests and there is continuous research being done on some of the eye issues that Pugs experience. I try to breed my Pugs to have inset eyes, not bulgy eyes. I don't think Pugs have any more issues than many other breeds. I have tried to breed Pugs that don't have breathing issues. Feeding a good balance of food can eliminate skin issues."

Your Veterinarian Is Your Partner

Working with a qualified veterinarian is critical to long-term and comprehensive healthcare. If you do not already have a vet, ask your breeder for a recommendation. If you purchased your pet outside your area, contact your local dog club and ask for referrals.

Make an appointment to tour the clinic and meet the vet. Be clear about the purpose of your visit and don't waste anyone's time! Go in with a set of prepared questions. Be sure to cover the following points:

- How long has this practice been in operation?
- How many vets are on staff?
- Are any of your doctors specialists?
- If not, to which doctors do you refer patients?
- What are your regular business hours?
- Do you recommend a specific emergency clinic?
- Do you have emergency hours?
- What specific medical services do you offer?
- Do you offer grooming services?
- Do you currently treat any Pugs?
- May I have an estimated schedule of fees?

Pay attention to all aspects of your visit, including how the facilities appear, and the demeanor of the staff. Things to look for include:

- how the staff interacts with clients

- the degree of organization or lack thereof
- indications of engagement with the clientele (office bulletin board, cards and photos displayed, etc.)
- quality of all visible equipment
- cleanliness and orderliness of the waiting area and back rooms
- prominent display of doctors' qualifications

These are only some suggestions. Go with your "gut." If the clinic and staff seems to "feel" right to you, trust your instincts. If not, no matter how well-appointed the practice may appear to be, visit more clinics before making a decision.

When you are comfortable with a vet practice, schedule a second visit to include your Pug puppy. Bring all the dog's medical records. Be ready to discuss completing vaccinations.

Routine exam procedures include temperature and a check of heart and lung function with a stethoscope. The vet will weigh and measure the puppy. These baseline numbers will help chart growth and physical progress. If you have specific questions, prepare them in advance.

BE AWARE: While the majority of veterinary organizations are well-meaning, they are businesses that need to make a profit, much of which can be from annual re-vaccinations and selling processed foods, both of which may not necessarily be in the best interests of your Pug.

Annie Sullivan of CASull Pugs: "New Pug people need to find a Veterinarian that's good with the "smooshy face" breeds, so plan on asking things like: How many Pugs do you have in your practice? How many Pugs have you spayed/neutered and done surgery on? Does a staff member stay with them until they come out of the anesthesia and the tube is removed?

"Keeping with the Veterinarian side of being a new Pug parent ... never give a rabies shot with any other shot! I've been told by most of the other breeders I've talked with that a Pug should never have a leptospirosis (or lepto as it's usually referred to). Plan on sitting at your Vet's office for at least 30 minutes after any shot is given to make sure they don't have an allergic reaction. A Pug can die quickly if an allergic reaction actually happens so you'll need your Vet to give them an antihistamine shot right away. An allergic reaction typically appears as a swollen nose roll and/or general puffy face and rubbing their face on anything and everything they can find. I always take a good look at my Pugs before they get the shot so I know exactly what their nose roll and face looks like before the shot. Sometimes a robust nose roll can make you think, "does that look like it's swelling to you?" and lead you into a panic!"

If a reaction occurs to a rabies vaccine the dog is going to go down quickly, and action should be taken immediately. Reactions to other vaccines do give a swollen face appearance. With any toy dog it is a good practice to wait in your vet's office for 15–20 minutes to make sure there is no reaction. With the advent of recombinant vaccines reactions are far fewer than in the past.

Photo Credit: Julia Ashton of Zobear Pugs.

Spaying and Neutering

Most reputable Pug sales are conducted by way of spay/neuter contracts stipulating that spaying or neutering is to be completed after the puppy has reached sexual maturity.

Females can get pregnant in old age—they don't go through a menopause. Spaying is the removal of her ovaries and womb (uterus).

Neutering is the removal of the male's testicles, also known as castration, in what is a routine operation. Yes, of course he will feel tender and slightly sore, but this will last only a few days.

Ask yourself, why wouldn't you have these procedures done unless of course you are planning to breed? Don't be swayed by popular misconceptions (myths) such as the operation will subdue or permanently affect his character and personality, or that the dog will gain weight. Remember that dogs are not humans; their need for sex is purely physical, caused by hormones that when removed will mean your dog does not desire or miss sex.

It is very important that the spaying/neutering procedures are not done until **sexual maturity** because there is ongoing emotional maturing that needs to take place. This maturation happens during the final phase of puppy adolescence (usually 12 months old) and helps to achieve healthy, balanced adult Pug behavior. Sexual maturity happens with a bitch puppy after a first menstrual cycle, often referred to as being "in heat" or "in season," and when the male dog is capable of siring pups.

A female Pug will have her menstrual cycle on average, every six or eight months, and this lasts usually 12–21 days. Her hormones will be raging, and through a sense of smell hundreds of times more powerful than ours, the male dogs from miles around will be on alert. You will notice some bleeding (spotting). This is perfectly normal.

Laura Libner of Lorarlar Pugs says: "More and more DVMs (Doctor of Veterinary Medicine) are now advocating that neutering a young Pug puppy is not in its best interest. With females, I would advocate spaying just before their first heat cycle, so around a year or so although this can vary on a case by case basis as there are exceptions to everything in medicine. For males, they could be neutered at a later age if necessary. I would say around a year to a year-and-a-half old would be best. Hormones are responsible for a large part of a dog's final development, growth plates closing, adrenal function, etc. and this encouragement to fix them earlier and earlier can be responsible for so many issues that crop up with dogs."

"It's also extremely important to have a DVM who is experienced and has an understanding of the challenges of sedation with a brachy breed and has references to back it up."

Christine Dresser DVM, Health Liaison, Pug Dog Club of America: "Average cost for spay in the US would be $300–$600; Neuter $200–$400. I sometimes recommend waiting on the girls through one heat cycle. They sometimes have very small vulvas and are prone to urinary tract infections. Having a heat cycle will likely increase the size and the risk for mammary cancer is still very low after one cycle."

Spaying and neutering procedures also carries health and behavioral benefits:

1. Neutering reduces the risk of prostatic disease or perianal tumors in male dogs.

2. The surgery may also lessen aggressive behaviors, territorial urine marking, and inappropriate mounting.

3. Spayed females have a diminished risk for breast cancer and no prospect of uterine or ovarian cancer.

4. There is no possibility of an unplanned or unwanted litter.

5. There are no mood swings related to hormones or issues (such as mess) around the bitch coming into season.

Vaccinations

If your Pug puppy is not immunized, then he is at risk from potentially fatal canine diseases because he has no protection. Contact with other dogs could occur at parks or at the vet's, so be very careful until he has received his first vaccinations. After birth, puppies receive immunity to many diseases from their mother's milk (this is called colostrum), but as they mature, this immunity fades.

Without immunization, your pup won't be covered under any pet insurance policy you may have taken out.

To give a balanced view, I will also point out that some breeders believe some Pugs are **'over-vaccinated'** and while very rare, there is the possibility of a reaction to the vaccine too. Certainly, Pugs are more susceptible than most other breeds.

A minor reaction could affect your Pug in ways such as making them sleepy, sneeze, irritable, and especially sore or developing a lump where injected. These should resolve in a few days.

A more severe reaction requiring immediate treatment would include vomiting, diarrhea, seizures, and a hypersensitivity reaction similar to that of a human **anaphylactic reaction**. Life-threatening anaphylactic reactions are very rare but not unheard of.

So what are the worst threats? There are **two deadly threats** that are the main focus of the initial vaccinations—distemper and parvovirus.

Distemper causes flu-like symptoms initially and progresses to severe painful neurological symptoms such as seizures and often ends in death. The virus is airborne so can be caught if your puppy comes into close proximity of an infected dog.

Parvovirus causes diarrhea and vomiting, often ending in death. The virus can be present in grass or on other surfaces for years.

A puppy's recommended core vaccinations via injection begin at eight weeks of age in the USA because if you vaccinate too soon you could interfere with maternal immunity.

A multivalent vaccination contains different vaccine antigens in a single dose; this is used by the majority of vets and is also less stressful for your Pug as it means fewer vet visits.

The most common combination vaccine given is known as DA2PP. The initials refer to the diseases included in the vaccine—Distemper, Adenovirus Type 1 (hepatitis), Adenovirus Type 2 (Respiratory Disease), Parainfluenza, and Parvo vaccine.

Recommended boosters occur at 12 and 16 weeks. Once this initial schedule has been completed, the debate opens up over the frequency of boosters. General practice is to give a distemper/parvo booster a year after the completion of their puppy series. After that, it depends on the individual vet, but usually a booster takes place every three years after the completion of the initial puppy series.

Every single dog should be protected against rabies. Puppies are usually given their first rabies vaccine after three months (some breeders wait until five months), then boosted again after a year and thereafter every three years.

There are some additional vaccines that are considered to be non-core or optional and should be administered based on what you decide with your vet.

Leptospirosis is a bacterial infection carried in the urine of mammals that dogs can contract if they drink infected standing water. In reality the number of cases are very low and many breeders believe the risk of adverse reactions to the vaccine outweigh the potential benefits.

In some forested regions in the US, a vaccine for Lyme disease starts at 16 weeks with a booster at 18 weeks.

Canine coronavirus also used to be part of some combination vaccines, but veterinarians no longer recommend it.

The Bordetella vaccine is the preventive against what is commonly known as kennel cough. It is usually required if your dog is staying at a boarding facility, groomer or overnight at a veterinarian's office but it is a personal choice as to whether this is necessary.

Christine Dresser DVM, Health Liaison, PDCA: "There is an oral form of Bordetella vaccine which is easy to administer and effective. I recommend Bord for dogs that are showing and competing since they are exposed to so many dogs from so many other areas."

Rabies is considered to have been eliminated within the UK so it is not a required vaccine for dogs unless you're planning on taking your dog on holiday with you to another EU country. Your dog will need to be at least 12 weeks old and already microchipped to have the jab. The injection is a requirement, among others, of getting a pet passport, which allows you to take your dog to and from another EU country.

Once your puppy has had their second set of vaccines at around 12 weeks, they should be safe to go into the outside world and play with other dogs.

Some of our breeders are in favor of a titer test. This is a straightforward blood test that measures a dog's antibodies to vaccine viruses. Titers accurately assess protection against the core diseases in dogs, enabling veterinarians to judge whether a booster vaccination is really necessary.

Christine Dresser DVM, Health Liaison, PDCA: "Titers do not guarantee immunity. Adequate titers are assumed to be protective but you would have to actually challenge the dog to know for sure."

TIP: On vaccinations, I would suggest people need to speak with their vets about local requirements, but be mindful of the latest World Small Animal Veterinary Association (WSAVA) advice, which has moved away from "annual boosters" for everything. Its membership is made up of global veterinary organizations: http://www.wsava.org/

Evaluating for Worms

Puppies purchased from a breeder are almost always parasite-free, because puppies are given their first dose of worming medication at around two weeks old, then again at four, six and eight weeks before they leave the litter.

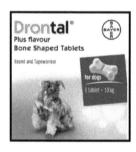

This is another reason to make sure you buy from a reputable breeder and not someone who doesn't know what they are doing. Worms are more common in rescue dogs, strays, and from "backyard breeders."

I have talked about taking your Pug to the vet within days of your purchase to get him health checked. A worm test is usually done then. These tests are important because some parasites, like tapeworm, may be life-threatening. Your vet will need a fecal sample for this purpose.

The main types of worms affecting puppies are **roundworm** and **tapeworm**. If the puppy tests positive, the standard treatment is a deworming agent with a follow-up dose after ten days.

Most vets usually recommend worming a puppy once a month until they are six months old, and then around every two or three months until they are adult dogs. At this stage opinion between vets does vary. Typically most would recommend deworming every three months, but it can depend on the level of risk in your local area. For pets at low risk for parasite exposure and people at low risk of infection, treatment is based on fecal examination results or, if fecal testing is not performed, once or twice yearly treatment is recommended. In high-risk households, fecal testing is recommended three to four times per year, with treatment based on results, or administration of routine preventive treatment at least two, but preferably three or four times per year.

Dangers to you: Roundworm can pass from a puppy to humans; in the most severe cases causing blindness or miscarriage in women. Make sure you wash your hands immediately after handling your puppy.

Christine Dresser DVM, Health Liaison, PDCA: "Of all the common worms we see, tapes are the least pathologic compared to hooks, whips and rounds. Tapes are mostly disgusting as they are the ones that can appear looking like a grain of dried rice around the anus or on the stool or crawl or move around the anus or on the furniture if that is where they land. Roundworm eggs are not visible without a microscope but the worms themselves, if they are vomited up or passed in stool are white, long and slender and often coil up.

"I do not routinely give worm medicine to dogs (such as worming monthly or yearly) with negative fecal results unless they are having some GI issue. Many of our monthly heartworm meds also contain medications against intestinal parasites."

Heartworm

Heartworm (*Dirofilaria Immitis*) is only present in certain parts of the world (usually the warmer ones), as it is dependent on the mosquitoes that transmit it through their bites. They are thin, long parasites that infest the muscles of the heart, where they block blood vessels and cause bleeding. Their presence can lead to heart failure and death.

Coughing and fainting, as well as an intolerance to exercise, are all symptoms of heartworm. Discuss heartworm prevention with your vet and decide on the best course of action to keep your pet safe.

There is another worm called *Angiostrongylus* (also known as French heartworm or lungworm), which is carried by slugs and snails. Dogs can be infected by eating them or licking at the trails. The worm can damage the lungs or lodge in the heart, as well as causing clotting disorders.

Christine Dresser DVM, Health Liaison, PDCA: "Heartworms are in the heart chambers and vessels, causing the heart to work harder and the walls of the vessels to thicken. Many dogs can have heartworm disease with no outward symptoms in the early stages of the disease. Many areas of the US recommend yearly blood tests and year round prevention."

Warning Signs of Illness in Your Pug

Often the signs of serious illness are subtle. Trust your instincts. If you think something is wrong, do not hesitate to consult with your vet.

- excessive and unexplained drooling
- excessive consumption of water and increased urination
- changes in appetite leading to weight gain or loss
- marked change in levels of activity
- disinterest in favorite activities
- stiffness and difficulty standing or climbing stairs
- sleeping more than normal
- shaking of the head
- any sores, lumps, or growths
- dry, red, or cloudy eyes
- any unusual odors
- excessive licking or scratching
- an eye that is squinting or partially closed
- straining to urinate or defecate

Diarrhea

Pug puppies, like all small dogs, are subject to digestive upsets. Puppies just will get into things they shouldn't, like human food or even the garbage. Diarrhea from these causes resolves within 24 hours. During that time, the puppy should have only small portions of dry food and no treats. Give the dog lots of fresh, clean water to guard against dehydration. If the loose, watery stools are still present after 24 hours, take your Pug to the vet.

The same period of watchful waiting applies to adult dogs. If episodic diarrhea becomes chronic, take a good look at your pet's diet. Chances are good that the dog is getting too much rich, fatty food and needs less fat and protein. Some dogs also do better eating small amounts of food several times a day rather than having two to three larger meals.

Many small dogs are allergic to chicken and turkey. A change in diet resolves their gastrointestinal upset immediately. Diets based on rabbit or duck are often used for dogs with such intolerances.

Either bacteria or a virus can cause diarrhea, which accompanies fever and vomiting. Parasites, in particular tapeworm and roundworm, may also be to blame. Usually parasitic diarrhea will be due to hooks, whips, rounds and coccidia.

Christine Dresser DVM, Health Liaison, PDCA: "Allergy testing for food intolerance is generally considered inaccurate. The only sure way to know is to do a well-designed food trial supervised by a vet, starting with a novel protein and carb source which can be difficult in today's market with food made from a wide variety of sources."

Understanding Vomiting

Dietary changes or the puppy "getting into something" can also cause vomiting. Again, this should resolve within 24 hours. If the dog tries to vomit but can't bring anything up, vomits blood, or can't keep water down, take your pet to the vet immediately.

Many Pug owners are concerned about their dogs not eating when their stomach is upset, but the real, main issue in this case is not drinking. Dehydration from vomiting can be fatal. It is possible that your dog may need intravenous fluids.

When your dog is vomiting, always have a good look around to identify what, if anything, the dog may have chewed and swallowed. This can be a huge benefit in targeting appropriate treatment.

Other potential culprits include: hookworm, roundworm, pancreatitis, diabetes, thyroid disease, kidney disease, liver disease, or a physical blockage.

Photo Credit: Julie Squire & Holly Attwood of Taftazini.

How to Treat Vomiting

If your Pug seems normal after it has vomited once or even twice, you can use the following treatment in the house as a practical solution.

1. For a period of six to eight hours at least, make sure that your dog has no contact with any source of food and water.

2. If during this period you see no signs of vomiting, you can allow your dog to have some water. Gradually increase the amount of water if your dog is able to hold the water down.

3. Wait for another 12 hours after allowing him to drink. If there is still no vomiting, you can start offering a small meal such as plain boiled and deboned chicken meat with white rice. If he eats and doesn't vomit, you can opt to give a bigger meal. Continue observing for a day or two as you start mixing in his regular food.

If you see that your Pug starts vomiting again in between treatment, it's best to go and see the veterinarian. The following symptoms require immediate treatment. Call a veterinarian right away.

1. Your dog's vomit is bright green in color. Green dye is usually found in some types of rodenticides (poisons) meant to kill rats and mice.

2. Your dog's vomit has red blood or ground coffee-like material. Both can be signs of gastrointestinal bleeding.

3. Your dog has shown repeated attempts at vomiting with each attempt producing nothing. It's a symptom of a potentially dangerous condition known as gastric dilatation volvulus.

4. There is pain in or enlargement of the dog's abdomen.

5. Urination is decreased. This can occur with signs of dehydration.

6. If your Pug is vomiting severely and has severe diarrhea, it can lead to dehydration.

7. Your Pug becomes lethargic and depressed, which shows that his body is seriously affected.

8. Your dog has projectile vomiting, which can be a sign of an obstructed gastrointestinal tract.

9. Your dog vomits frequently, which can make him debilitated. This is usually seen among puppies and older dogs.

Vomiting and Its Diagnosis

It is advised that cases of repetitive, prolonged, and severe vomiting need to be placed under a thorough investigation.

Veterinarians are highly capable of reaching a diagnosis on the underlying condition behind your dog's vomiting by doing certain procedures. These include getting information on the health history and lifestyle of your dog, conducting a physical examination, and potentially running several tests such as biopsies, ultrasound imaging, urinalysis, fecal analysis, blood test, X-rays, and other diagnostic tests. You can also bring a sample of your dog's stool and vomit, which may help in the diagnostic process.

What You Can Do to Prevent Vomiting

While it is true that several causes of vomiting among dogs have no ways of prevention, there are some things you can do to help:

1. Keep an eye on an overly inquisitive dog, particularly when you are out and about. You may want to keep a basket muzzle handy to make sure that your dog doesn't eat anything that is non-edible.

2. Make sure that your Pug does not scavenge. Scavenging is said to be the root cause of gastroenteritis. It's also believed to increase the risk of toxin exposure and ingestion of foreign bodies.

3. Never allow your dog to consume table scraps. This is because there are some human foods which have dangerous content and therefore should never be fed to dogs. Some types of food that are not "dog-friendly" include macadamia nuts, garlic, onions, chocolate, and grapes.

4. Never give bones to your dog that can break into sharp shards. Otherwise, you can allow the large bone types such as the knuckles or femurs so long as they are uncooked.

5. Make sure that your dog's toys are safe and not a choking hazard.

6. Avoid a sudden change in your Pug's diet. If you need to make changes, do it gradually. Sudden changes in your dog's dietary habit have been attributed to be the common cause of intestinal upset.

Lung Lobe Torsion

This is a rare and seemingly random condition where the lobe of the lung twists restricting blood flow. Unlike humans, dogs and cats have separate lung lobes (Pugs have three right lung lobes and two left lung lobes), which make them more prone to undergoing torsion (twisting).

As fluid accumulates in the chest, the normal lung lobes collapse, and the dog develops shortness of breath. The torsed lung lobe dies releasing toxins into the body. Look out for warning signs of shortness of breath (rapid, shallow breathing) and lethargy.

The diagnosis is based on clinical signs, physical examination, chest X-ray findings, and analysis of the fluid from the chest cavity. Surgery is recommended to remove the torsed lung lobe. This is typically performed via an incision that is made on the side of the chest. After the lung lobe is removed, a tube is placed through the chest wall and into the chest cavity. The surgical incision is then closed. The chest tube is placed to allow for evaluation of fluid and air from the chest cavity. This tube is typically removed two to three days after surgery.

Christine Dresser DVM, Health Liaison, PDCA: "Club members started telling me about their experience with LLT years ago and my first question (never having seen it in practice or in my dogs) was what did the dog do? Was it really sick? The answer in every case was the Pug was quiet and had a decreased appetite. Then one of my 15-month-old, group winning black males started acting quiet and didn't want to eat. My first thought was he was having a GI disturbance—wrong. Blood was normal but the chest films were not.

"All dogs have two left and three right lobes. Almost every other breed that experiences LLT will have the right middle lobe spontaneously twist. They have a 50:50 chance in surgery according to the boarded surgeon who cut my dog. The Pugs have their left cranial lobe twist and they have a very high chance for full recovery. The signs are very subtle. You would think they would at least cough but there really aren't any obvious signs such a bad thing is happening. The radiographic signs can also look like pneumonia and I know of a Pug who was followed for a week before going to surgery. When I called the specialty hospital to set up an appointment with a surgeon, the receptionist was interpreting it as an emergency and said come right in but I told her the dog was stable and we waited for an appointment the next day. It is costly—figure on $5000–7000.

"Pugs are over-represented and we don't know why. Some have speculated it is due to body shape but they are not built so differently and that explanation is not satisfactory.

"There is no issue in the chest prior to the lobe twisting. There can then be some bleeding or weeping of fluid, but again, at least with Pugs, they sure don't let you know what might be going on."

Mast Cell Tumor Disease

This is a form of cancer (of the mast cells) to which the Pug is susceptible to as well as Boxers, Bulldogs and Boston Terriers.

Mast cells reside in many tissues in the body, especially the skin, lungs, mouth, nose, conjunctiva of the eyes and digestive tract. They are part of the body's immune system playing an important role in allergies and defense against worm infestations.

Look for a lump or swelling on or in your Pug's skin and get a vet to perform an aspiration biopsy of the lump.

Grade 1 tumors are the least likely to be highly malignant and grade 3 are the most likely to be malignant. Around 90% of dogs are reported to have long term survival after a grade 1 diagnosis.

Allergies

Like humans, dogs suffer from allergies. Allergies can come from a number of sources, not just pollen. Food, airborne particles, and materials that touch the skin can all cause negative reactions.

One of the commonest causes of allergies in dogs is house dust mites, and it is a good idea to suggest having the dog tested for causes so that the vet can advise on ways to control allergies.

Owners tend to notice changes in behavior that suggest discomfort like itching. **Common symptoms** include chewing or biting of the tail, stomach, or hind legs, or licking of the paws.

In reaction to inhaled substances, the dog will sneeze, cough, or experience watering eyes. Ingested substances may lead to vomiting or diarrhea. Dogs can also suffer from rashes or a case of hives. Your poor Pug can be just as miserable as you are during an allergy attack. If the reaction occurs in the spring or fall, the likely culprit is **seasonal pollen** or, in the case of hot weather, **fleas**.

If your dog is allergic to something inside your home, he'll have year-round symptoms. If he's reacting is to something outdoors, it could very well be a seasonal problem and in this case **foot soaks** are good to do because chances are that the allergen is coming inside on their feet, and this stops it spreading round the house.

Consider investing in an **air purifier** to control dust mites and ensure all cleaning products are non-toxic — these could also be the cause of the allergy: Vacuum and change bedding more frequently.

Flea allergy dermatitis (FAD) is a very common condition affecting dogs. It is not the bite of the flea that causes most of the itching; it's the reaction to the saliva.

Consider whether your Pug is over-vaccinated or over-medicated, as these can affect your pet's immune system and set the stage for allergic conditions. The right balance of gut bacteria is crucial for health, and there is evidence that antibiotics can wipe out good bacteria (as well as the bad).

Your vet may recommend bathing the dog in cool, soothing water, which not only feels pleasurable but washes away the allergens. Special diets are also extremely helpful. Relieving symptoms without addressing the source of the problem is a short-term fix to what can become a lifelong health problem. Usually, the more your Pug gets exposure to an irritant, the more his sensitivity and reaction increases.

For acne-like chin rashes, switch to stainless steel, glass, or ceramic food dishes. Plastic feeding dishes cause this rash, which looks like blackheads surrounded by inflamed skin. Wash the dog's face in clear, cool water and ask the vet for an antibiotic cream to speed the healing process.

Connie J. Dunham of MtnAire Pugs: "Allergies are a tough issue to deal with. I had allergies as a child and couldn't have a dog, period, and no other animals in fact! Pugs are not allergen free. Most allergies stem from the dander in dogs' skin, not from shed hair. There are a few breeds that people with allergies can tolerate fairly quickly. As most people grow up, at some point they can be exposed to a particular dog and can develop a resistance to allergic reactions to that dog. That's what I found as I became a teen. We got a small short-haired dog and I could play with her and not have any reactions but if I was exposed to other dogs, I would still have allergic reactions.

"There are many medications available now that can help people tolerate pets. This would be an issue to discuss with an allergy doctor if a family really wanted to indulge in a Pug and had a family member who might have issues. There are pathways to developing the resistance necessary to add a dog to an affected family. They have found that exposing very young infants to dogs and cats helps to stop the incidence of allergies in children. This might be helpful for future children in the mix!"

Pam Donaldson of Highland/Kendoric Pugs: "We see many Pugs coming into our Pug Rescue of New England with skin allergies; some quite severe causing alopecia (hair loss) and darkening and thickening of skin in the affected areas. I have never had this problem with my own Pugs so my guess is that this is a result of poor breeding practices and something a person searching for a puppy should ask a breeder about."

General Signs of Illness

Any of the following symptoms can point to a serious medical problem. Have your pet evaluated for any of these behaviors. Don't wait out of fear that you are just being an alarmist. Vets can resolve most medical problems in dogs if treatment starts at the first sign of illness.

Coughing and/or Wheezing

Occasional coughing is not a cause for concern, but if it goes on for more than a week, a vet visit is in order. A cough may indicate:

- kennel cough
- heartworm
- cardiac disease
- bacterial infections
- parasites
- tumors
- allergies

The upper respiratory condition called 'Kennel Cough Syndrome' presents with dry hacking. It is a form of canine bronchitis caused by warm, overcrowded conditions with poor ventilation. In most cases, kennel cough resolves on its own, but do take it seriously, as it can lead to fatal bronchopneumonia in an older dog, and in dogs with an underlying heart condition, it can lead to heart failure.

Infections can last up to six weeks. Your Pug should be kept isolated until several days after they stop coughing. Any dog that has come into contact with an affected dog should also be isolated, as they may transmit the kennel cough to other dogs. Consult with your veterinarian. The doctor may prescribe a cough suppressant or suggest the use of a humidifier to soothe your pet's irritated airways.

When the cause of a cough is unclear, the vet will take a full medical history and order tests, including blood work and X-rays. Fluid may also be drawn from the lungs for analysis. Among other conditions, the doctor will be attempting to rule out heartworm.

If your dog has a heart murmur, they may cough. Get a chest X-ray to see if the heart is enlarged.

Dental Care

Thanks to their short brachycephalic snout, Pugs have less room to accommodate the standard 42 teeth. As an adaptation, the Pug's teeth are smaller, but overcrowding and breakage can still be a problem with the breed.

Regular dental exams at the vet's are an important part of preventive health care for these dogs. It's not unusual for molars to be removed to prevent shifting and slanting of the front and middle teeth. Although an underbite is normal for a Pug, if the lower jaw overextends to a serious degree, it can interfere with eating and the placement of the tongue. In these cases, more extensive corrective surgery may be needed.

Chewing is a dog's only means of maintaining his teeth. Many of our canine friends develop dental problems early in life because they don't get enough of this activity. Not all dogs are prone to cavities.

Most do suffer from accumulations of plaque and associated gum diseases. Often, severe halitosis (bad breath) is the first sign that something is wrong.

With dental problems, gingivitis develops first and, if unaddressed, progresses to periodontitis. Warning signs of gum disease include:

- a reluctance to finish meals
- extreme bad breath
- swollen and bleeding gums
- irregular gum line
- plaque build-up
- drooling and/or loose teeth

Pugs are prone to developing gum and tooth disease because their jaws tend to be small and often their teeth are crowded. The bacterial gum infection periodontitis causes inflammation, gum recession, and possible tooth loss. It requires treatment with antibiotics to prevent a spread of the infection to other parts of the body. Symptoms include:

- pus at the gum line
- loss of appetite
- depression
- irritability
- pawing at the mouth
- trouble chewing
- loose or missing teeth
- gastrointestinal upset

Treatment begins with a professional cleaning. This procedure may also involve root work, descaling, and even extractions.

With proliferating gum disease, the gums overgrow the teeth, causing inflammation and infection. Other symptoms include:

- thickening and lengthening of the gums
- bleeding
- bad breath
- drooling
- loss of appetite

The vet will prescribe antibiotics, and surgery is usually required.

David Johnson (DVM) and Judith Johnson (CVT) of Foursquare Pugs: "Dental care is another piece of the Pug puzzle. Pugs mouths are shaped in a way that is really easy to ignore the trouble that may be brewing. Not only are all brachycephalic breeds hard to examine, but because of the shape of their jaws there is just not enough room for their teeth to be set properly. Their teeth placement is such that it traps food and enhances the chance for dental disease. Good cleaning practices should be introduced at an early age, and if this is just not for you, then they need to see a veterinarian for dental checkups."

Diabetes

Canines can suffer from three types of diabetes: insipidus, diabetes mellitus, and gestational diabetes. All point to malfunctioning endocrine glands and are often linked to poor diet. Larger dogs are in a higher risk category.

- In cases of **diabetes insipidus**, low levels of the hormone vasopressin create problems with the regulation of blood glucose, salt, and water.

- **Diabetes mellitus** is more common and dangerous. It is divided into Types I and II. The first develops in young dogs and may be referred to as "juvenile." Type II is more prevalent in adult and older dogs. All cases are treated with insulin.

- **Gestational diabetes** occurs in pregnant female dogs and requires the same treatment as diabetes mellitus. Obese dogs are at greater risk.

Abnormal insulin levels interfere with blood sugar levels. Any dog that is obese is at a higher risk for developing diabetes.

Symptoms of Canine Diabetes

All of the following behaviors are signs that a dog is suffering from canine diabetes:

- excessive water consumption
- excessive and frequent urination
- weight gain (or loss) for no apparent reason
- lethargy/uncharacteristic laziness

It is possible your Pug may display no symptoms whatsoever. Diabetes can be slow to develop, so the effects may not be immediately noticeable. Regular check-ups help to catch this disease, which can be fatal even when you do not realize that anything is wrong.

As part of a diabetes management program, the vet will recommend diet changes, including special food. Your dog may need insulin injections. Although this may sound daunting, your vet will train you to administer the shots.

A dog with diabetes can live a full and normal life. Expect regular visits to the vet to check for heart and circulatory problems.

Canine Eye Care

Check your dog's eyes on a regular schedule to avoid problems like clogged tear ducts. Also, many dogs suffer from excessive tearing, which can stain the fur around the eyes and down the muzzle.

As a part of good grooming, keep the corners of your pet's eyes and the muzzle free of mucus to prevent bacterial growth. If your dog is prone to mucus accumulation, ask your vet for sterile eyewash or gauze pads. Also consider having the dog tested for environmental allergies.

While the Pug's large prominent eyes gives it the unique look that many people cannot resist falling for, it also results in more eye issues than most other breeds. You will need to check them regularly for abnormal redness, inflammation, discharge or signs of a half or completely closed eye.

Dogs love to hang their heads out of car windows, but this can result in eye injuries and serious infection from blowing debris. There is a product called Doggles, which are protective goggles for dogs in a range of colors and sizes for less than $20 / £12 per pair, but I would really **advise against** allowing your dog to let it stick its head out the window in the first place, as it is a dangerous habit.

Eye Ulcers in Pugs

We have a special article for you by **Belinda Goyarts of Raevon Pugs.** This is her own personal experiences with eye ulcers and the information has been kindly checked over by Dr Chloe Hardman BVSc, FACVf, Opthal, Melbourne Eye Vet — Victoria, Australia.

Having run a nationwide Pug rescue for many years, I have become rather more acquainted with eye ulcers than I ever wanted to. Pugs are filled with boundless energy and a high level of curiosity, resulting in an extremely active and energetic breed of dog that just has to investigate every single thing in life.

This is great — however, with a standard that calls for eyes to be 'dark, very large and globular in shape' I sometimes wish that my beloved breed had more of a couch potato disposition. I also find that Australian conditions (hot, dry and dusty) are not conducive to owning Pugs—I'm quite sure UK Pug owners do not have as many day to day challenges with dust, prickly Yukka plants and dry air from constant air conditioning.

Pugs, Boxers (and other dogs prone to eye problems) are prone to getting ulcers from scratches (plants/sticks/playing with another dog), or a bit of soap in the eye from bathing, or from lying beside a fan heater; a hot dusty day can result in the cornea (eye surface) drying out from dust, eyelashes rubbing on the surface, or in the case of my guys at times, it seems just breathing.

General practitioner veterinary clinics do a good job with eyes in many cases. However, I have learned enormous amounts from the actual eye care specialists—Melbourne Eye Vets—and their treatments are far more proactive, and as a result, eyes are healed in a far shorter time frame, resulting in less pain and more eyes saved.

This article is written so that Pug owners can have a better understanding of eye ulcers and how to diagnose quickly and treat them immediately, thereby, in a high percentage of cases, fixing the problem in a couple of days, rather than weeks, or worse, losing an eye altogether.

Danger signs to watch for

The very first sign of an ulcer is generally excessive 'blinking' of the eye with some excess tears. If slightly worse, the eye can be squinting, and the lids look a little swollen. A trip to the vet and staining of the eye with a green dye will reveal the ulcer in its various stages of development.

The cornea (eye surface) is 0.7 mm thick and has several layers: the epithelium (surface—seven cell layers thick), the stroma (collagen in about 100 layers—like an onion), the endothelium, and Descemet's membrane.

A very shallow ulcer (often just epithelial depth) can be barely visible, but may develop a bluish clouding over a portion of the eye from fluid retention (edema) due to inflammation. Sometimes ulcers can look like a white pinprick, a white scratch, or even a larger white area as big as a flattened cotton tip bud. Deeper ulcers can look like a hole or a divet (these involve the stroma). Very deep ulcers look like a deep hole, and the inner membrane can bulge = Descemetocele. These can perforate, resulting in a collapse of the eye.

You've ascertained that there is an ulcer—now what?

The major, very serious problem with ulcers is that quite apart from being painful, **they can get infected very, very quickly, which is where the BIG problems start.**

Treated superficial ulcers can sit on the eye surface and heal at a normal rate, the big issue is to clear them up quickly, as the longer they sit there, the more chance they have of becoming infected, and it is the infection that will rapidly eat through the surface layers of the cornea and result in perforation, quickly reaching the gelatinous filling of the eye, which can then leak out of the ulcerated hole. You have then progressed from a fairly easy-to-fix problem to a major issue involving surgery, grafts and/or possible loss of the eye.

Initial treatment

1. Confirmation of the ulcer through staining with a Fluorescein strip. It is a good idea to have a look yourself once the ulcer is outlined clearly through the staining by the veterinarian, so that you can note if it is getting smaller/bigger after a day or two when you are at home.

2. Immediate prescription of antibiotics and anti-inflammatory drugs.

3. Place an Elizabethan collar so they are not able to rub the eye.

It is imperative that antibiotics be given in two forms:

• Chlorsig antibiotic drops: These are antibiotic drops that are administered 3—6 times daily to the eye. These drops are excellent as they are broad spectrum. However they only stay in the eye for a short period of time before being washed away by tears. For this reason, it is essential that another form of antibiotic be administered that will have a longer and more lasting effect against possible infection:

• Doxycycline tablets (oral antibiotics): Doxycycline is **the best form of antibiotics** to use in eye injuries as it concentrates in the dogs' tears, and flushes over the cornea through the tear ducts 24 hours a day. Just as importantly, it has recently been found that Doxycycline, apart from fighting infection, promotes the healing of the cornea AND is anti-inflammatory. Worth its weight in gold!

Anti-inflammatory drugs

• Carprieve or Prolet (or similar) tablets should be prescribed — they are anti-inflammatory and also offer effective pain relief.

• Optimmune ointment 3 x daily — this ointment acts like false tears and lubricates and protects the eye, has anti-inflammatory properties, and promotes normal tear production/healthy tear film.

If corneal ulcers become infected, or resist healing, more potent antibiotics should be used e.g. fortified gentamicin drops (gentamicin ointment and drops not strengthened by adding extra gentamicin drug are of little use). Initially, these drops need to be used 10 + times daily until the infection has resolved (may take 7+ days).

• An alternative is Ocuflox (ofloxacin), which is even more potent.

On arriving home

DO NOT LEAVE THE CLINIC WITHOUT AN ELIZABETHAN COLLAR; this will prevent your Pug from rubbing the very delicate cornea. Be sure to keep him inside out of the wind and dust, until blinking and inflammation have disappeared.

Gently wipe any mucous away from the eye with sterile (or boiled) water before applying drops and ointments. **DO NOT RUB CREAMS INTO THE EYE** as you risk causing further trauma to the site. Apply the cream from approximately 1 cm away, and it will dissolve over the corneal surface. With smaller ulcers that have not become infected, you should notice a change within 24 hours, and an almost clear corneal surface within three days.

The ulcer is not healing

Sometimes the position of the ulcer is so central, or so minimal in size, that blood vessels are not reaching out far enough to heal it. This is what you would then call an 'indolent' ulcer, meaning that, although it is not necessarily getting bigger, it is not healing either. The danger lies in that the longer the ulcer is present, the greater the chance of infection occurring, so it needs to be dealt with quickly and effectively.

To encourage healing, vets can put anesthetic drops on the cornea and then lightly debride (rub) the surface of the ulcer with a cotton tip bud to remove any unhealthy tissue that was not properly attached to the cornea (due to the presence of the ulcer). This loose tissue can have a delaying or negative effect in healing.

However, if the vet debrides the ulcer and its edges peel back, surgery is generally needed in the form of a **grid keratotomy**.

Grid Keratotomy

This is only done to VERY SUPERFICIAL ulcers and needs to be performed under a general anesthetic. Eye specialists may be able to perform this with the patient awake under a topical anesthetic in the consult room depending on how large the ulcer becomes when the edges are peeled off and the unhealthy epithelium (skin layer) is removed.

A grid keratotomy involves taking a fine hypodermic needle and etching grid lines on the surface of the cornea over and around the ulcer. The grid lines allow healthy cells surrounding the ulcer to move along the channels into the unhealthy section of the cornea, thereby promoting healing.

To protect the site, the third eyelid can then be raised and attached to the upper eyelid with stitches. In some cases, the inside of the third eyelid can be scarified (shallow cuts/scraping performed) to allow the resulting blood flow directly on to the cornea to stimulate healing. The raising of the third eyelid will promote healing, and protect the eye from further trauma.

In the case of a deep hole/ulcer

Deep holes/ulcers require **a conjunctival pedicle graft** — surgery will lift up an area of healthy conjunctiva (eye surface) and graft it over the unhealthy area. This is sewn into the ulcer bed. To protect the eye, a **temporary tarsorrhaphy** is done (a couple of stitches closing the upper and lower eyelid at the outer/inner corner closest to the graft site). These stitches are removed once the graft has reduced in size and the eye is returning to its more normal state.

Greater eye traumas — signs to watch for

Initial symptoms of an ulcer can be blinking and excess tears. It is easy to keep an eye on this on a daily basis. After surgery has been done however, and the eye itself is covered by the third eyelid flap, it is not as easy to keep an eye on progress.

Initial symptoms of problems/greater eye injuries: inflamed eye area, redness, swelling, the dog averting its head from light, pulling its head away from the eye area as if trying to escape pain, sleeping a lot (an excellent sign to watch for when the third eye lid is sewn up — the dog gets so tired from the pain that it actually sleeps far more than is normal).

Another excellent pain indicator is to compare pupils (if you do not have a third eyelid flap raised). The normal healthy eye will have a pupil that contracts with light and dilates back again when you remove the direct light. An eye in distress will generally have a pin prick pupil, as the eye spasms in pain and prevents the pupil from dilating.

In spasming pinprick cases, vets will administer Atropine hourly for a few hours to relieve the spasms (on top of all the other treatments). Atropine causes the pupil to dilate to its fullest for 24 hours or more, making the eye extremely sensitive to light (as it cannot contract) so it is most important that when Atropine is being administered, you **keep your dog in a darkened room.**

Theories/alternative remedies

I have discussed at length with the specialists the alternative remedies used by owners, and several come to mind immediately:

Breeders have at times praised the use of milk, cod liver oil and/or serum taken from the affected dog as a treatment for ulcers. Whilst specialists did not discount these remedies, they did make a good point, which is that ulcers easily and rapidly become infected, which means they MUST be treated with antibiotics. Cod liver oil and serum may help with healing, but only after the danger of infection has been removed.

Emergency Eye Kit

Living and travelling with Pugs means having emergency eye kits situated in various places. I always have one in the car, the show trailer, the caravan and in the house. I am not in any way advising readers not to seek veterinary advice; however, I have found that if I am at a dog show, and miles away from my vet on a public holiday, I can at least commence treatment, which has no adverse effect on my dogs and will provide pain relief and possible prevention of infection. My emergency kits are made up of:

• Fluorescein staining strips
• Carprieve or Prolet tablets (pain relief and anti-inflammatory)
• Doxycycline (antibiotics)
• Chlorsig (antibiotic drops)
• Optimmune (lubrication and anti-inflammatory)
• Sterile water sachets (x 2) for debris removal
• Cotton pads (non-fibrous)
• Atropine drops—these drops are an **extremely important** part of your eye kit. They dilate the pupil and have two functions:

1) They stop the eye spasming in pain and

2) In the cases of a deep ulcer, which is looking like it is on its way to perforating during your drive to the vet,—the atropine drops will have caused the pupil to dilate, which in turn can potentially plug the hole caused by perforation, and prevent too much loss of pressure before you get to the veterinarian.

I keep all these items in each kit, and have found the small flattish Tupperware containers to be excellent as they store in small places easily, such as the car console.

This article only covers some of the more common occurrences that can crop up on a daily basis—and is just information that I have accumulated over the years and hopefully can be of some use.

By Belinda Goyarts - http://www.raevonpugs.com

Photo Credit: Heidi Merkli of Bugaboo Reg'd.

Conjunctivitis

Conjunctivitis, otherwise known as "pink eye", is the most common eye infection seen in dogs. It presents with redness around the eyes and a green or yellow discharge. Antibiotics will treat the infection. The dreaded "cone of shame" collar then prevents more injury from scratching during healing.

What are the various types and symptoms of conjunctivitis?

1. The conjunctiva is described as the moist tissue that acts like a covering of the frontal area of the eyeball, as well as a lining around the eyelids. Conjunctivitis occurs when there is redness in the eye's moist tissues.

2. There is the unusual habit of squinting or spasmodic blinking.

3. Your dog's eyes produce a discharge, which is either clear or has mucus/pus content.

4. There is swelling as a result of the build-up of fluid in the eye's moist tissues.

5. Follicle formation gives the moist tissue area of the eyelids a cobblestone appearance. Follicles are actually an accumulation of lymphoid tissues that are said to have lymphocytes.

What causes conjunctivitis?

Conjunctivitis may be caused by several factors that range from viral, bacterial, to cancer and more. Viral causes of conjunctivitis have been solely attributed to the so-called **canine distemper** virus.

Bacterial causes can classify conjunctivitis as either a primary condition or neonatal. The latter involves newborn inflammation around the moist tissues in the eye area caused by accumulation of discharge. The discharge is usually seen before the dog's eyelids open or before they separate.

At times, conjunctivitis has also been linked to signs of cancer. Some of these signs include tumors (rare); lesions; inflammation of the border that is found between the cornea and the sclera; and presence of nodules that appear like a pink mass.

Conjunctivitis can also be a secondary condition brought on by various diseases and environmental causes. These include lash diseases; lid diseases; lack of normal tear film or dry eye; irritation from eye medications, chemicals or dust; foreign body in the eye's moist tissues; glaucoma; anterior uveitis; and ulcerative keratitis.

Conjunctivitis and its diagnosis

In making a diagnosis, the veterinarian would first look for evidence of other eye diseases. This is to find out whether conjunctivitis is also evident in other parts of the eye apart from the conjunctiva. An eye exam is usually conducted wherein various methods of examination are used.

One method uses the so-called "fluorescein stain," wherein the surface of the eye is spread with fluorescein. This allows ulcers, scratches, and foreign materials to appear more visible under the light. This type of method is an ideal way to rule out ulcerative keratitis. The dog's lids or eyelashes are also examined thoroughly to check for the presence of foreign materials.

Eye pressure is also determined in order to diagnose glaucoma while the nasal cavity is sometimes flushed out to diagnose the presence of disease in the area.

If the eye brings out a discharge, the vet will perform a culture in order to determine the components of the discharge, which can indicate an infection. Microscopic examination may also be conducted by collecting a biopsy of conjunctiva cells.

Lastly, the vet may run a skin test if there is a reason to suspect skin allergies as the underlying cause of conjunctivitis.

Cataracts

A cataract is the clouding or darkening in the lens of the eye that results from accumulated proteins leading to blurred vision.

Surgery is the only permanent solution for this problem, though many Pugs adapt well to changes in vision—even total loss of vision. However, you should have your dog's cataracts checked by a veterinarian in any case, to rule out secondary complications.

n most cases, the vet will watch, but not treat, cataracts. The condition does not affect your pet's life in a severe way. Dogs adapt well to the senses they do have, so diminished vision is not as problematic as it would be for us.

Glaucoma

Glaucoma in dogs is a health condition characterized by pressure that is placed on the eye, which causes the latter to suffer from inadequate fluid drainage. When the condition reaches a chronic state or it continues without any treatment, the dog can experience blindness as a result of the permanent damage to his optic nerve.

The bad news is that 40 percent of affected dogs will experience blindness in the affected eye within just the first year of being diagnosed with the condition. This is particularly true whether the dog received medical or surgical treatment.

What are the types and symptoms of glaucoma in dogs?

Glaucoma in dogs has two main types: primary and secondary. Primary open angle glaucoma Pug type (POAG) is an eye disorder causing a build-up of pressure in the eye.

Symptoms of sudden occurrence of glaucoma include:

1. Loss of vision
2. Dilated pupil or the pupil being unresponsive to light
3. Cloudy appearance at the eye's front part
4. Unnatural blinking of the eye
5. Blood vessels in the eye's whites appearing obviously red
6. Receding eyeball back into the dog's head
7. High pressure felt within the eye

Glaucoma, in the long term, is said to develop into certain advanced diseases. These include advanced degeneration within the dog's eye, obvious vision loss, and *bupthalmos*, or enlargement of the eyeball.

Secondary glaucoma in dogs is more common compared to primary glaucoma and is said to be caused by secondary eye infections. Symptoms include the following:

1. Suspected circular sticking of the iris's edge to the lens
2. Suspected sticking of the iris either to the lens or to the cornea
3. Suspected pupil constriction
4. Inflammatory debris in the front part of the eye
5. Cloudy appearance at the front part of the eye
6. Unusual redness of the blood vessels in the eyes' whites
7. High pressure found within the eye

Other notable symptoms of glaucoma include less desire to interact or play; obvious change in attitude; absence of appetite; and headaches.

Glaucoma and its diagnosis

In order to have an accurate diagnosis, you should be able to provide a comprehensive health history of your dog. This will include symptoms that have occurred as far as you can remember and notable incidents that could have contributed to the condition. One example would be injuries to the eye regardless of whether they are minor or major.

When conducting a physical examination, the vet will use a tonometer on the eye's surface in order to test the pressure within. If glaucoma has been diagnosed as a sudden disease, the vet will advise you to take your dog to a veterinary ophthalmologist. The latter will conduct a detailed examination on both eyes. This includes using gonioscopy, which is the method of measuring the eye's anterior in order to evaluate its filtration angles.

They will also perform the so-called **electroretinography** for the purpose of determining whether the eye will remain blind even after treatment. On the other hand, abnormalities in the eye are usually detected through ultrasound and X-rays in secondary diseases.

When the dog has been diagnosed with glaucoma in one eye, certain measures are taken to protect and prevent the unaffected eye from suffering the same condition.

Cherry Eye

Dogs have a unique eye anatomy. They have up to six eyelids, with each eye having three. These are the upper eyelid, the lower lid, and the third eyelid, which we seldom see. Otherwise known as nictitating membranes, the dog's third eyelids normally lie beneath the lower lids.

Both the upper and lower eyelids function very much like human eyelids. The third eyelids act like an extra layer of eye protection in dogs. It's like a wipe that helps in keeping the eye clear of dust and debris. It also has a tear gland that increases moisture in the dog's eye by around 35 percent.

The dog's third eyelids also have glands that are found in the corner of

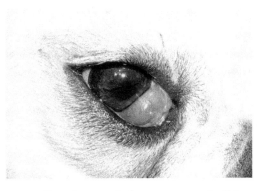

the eye right next to his nose. Sometimes the gland slips out of place and appears to be bulging. This bulge, which is similar to a red or pinkish blob, is what's known as "cherry eye".

Although the exact causes of cherry eye are not well understood, there are certain things about it that we should be aware of.

1. Cherry eye is neither a true medical emergency nor a life-threatening condition. Dogs with cherry eye feel a number of discomforts. This includes inflammation, irritation, eye redness (conjunctivitis), and others. To relieve the discomfort, dogs should be treated promptly at the veterinarian clinic. The move will also help in preventing permanent ocular damage.

2. It is possible that the cherry eye condition will correct by itself in a couple of weeks. However, waiting for this to happen can be frustrating. The longer time that the gland is out of place, the bigger it becomes due to swelling. Since it is bigger, it is harder to reposition it.

Moreover, there's a huge chance that the condition will occur again. If left untreated, it can later lead to a more serious problem.

3. Dogs that are younger, around six weeks to two years, are more likely to be seen with a cherry eye. While any breed can develop the condition, cherry eye is more commonly found in Neapolitan Mastiffs, Miniature Poodles, Lhasa Apsos, Pekingese, Pugs, Shih Tzus, Shar-Peis, Cocker Spaniels, Bulldogs, Bloodhounds, Newfoundlands, and Boston Terriers.

I personally have seen some as early as eight weeks and as late as ten years of age. Treatment may consist of a simple application of an appropriate ophthalmic ointment and reduction of the prolapse by your veterinarian. The two methods for surgical treatment are:

1. TACKING — a properly trained veterinarian surgically sutures the gland back into its normal position. The tear production is not altered with this method. There is a chance that the cherry eye will pop back out. Some resources have it at 10–30% reoccurrence rate.

2. REMOVAL — this method is quick, and usually a cautery procedure is used. The gland is removed.

Canine Arthritis

Dogs, like humans, can suffer from arthritis, which may develop in the presence of hip or elbow dysplasia as a secondary complication. Arthritis is a debilitating degeneration of the joints and is common in larger breeds. As the cartilage in the joints breaks down, the action of bone rubbing on bone creates considerable pain. In turn, the animal's range of motion becomes restricted.

Standard treatments do not differ from those used for humans. Aspirin addresses pain and inflammation, while supplements like glucosamine work on improving joint health. Environmental aids, like steps and ramps, ease the strain on the affected joints and help pets stay active.

Arthritis also occurs as a natural consequence of aging. Management focuses on making your pet comfortable and facilitating ease of motion.

Some dogs become so crippled that their humans buy mobility carts for them.

Hip and Elbow Dysplasia

Any breed can be susceptible to hip dysplasia. This defect prevents the leg bones from fitting properly into the hip joint. It is a painful condition that causes limping in the hindquarters. The condition may be inherited, or the consequence of injury and aging.

The standard treatment is anti-inflammatory medication. Some cases need surgery and even a full joint replacement. Surgical intervention for this defect carries a high success rate, allowing your dog to live a full and happy life.

Christine Dresser DVM, Health Liaison, PDCA: "According to the Orthopedic Foundation for Animals, Pugs have had the highest rate of hip dysplasia in all breeds for the last 2 years; prior to that we were ranked second to Bulldogs. There is also a fair amount of elbow dysplasia reported, but the accumulated data are seriously skewed by a large related group of dogs that were almost uniformly affected. Affected Pugs will often develop arthritis and not be able to jump as they once did. They can be maintained on anti-inflammatory medications and might also be surgical candidates for either a total hip replacement or a femoral head osteotomy. There are many factors that contribute to hip dysplasia and it has proved to be very hard to reduce or eliminate as not all breeders will test for it. Breeders should be screening their breeding stock and removing severely affected dogs from the breeding program. Nutrition research by Purina has indicated that puppies should transition to adult dog food early (8–10 weeks), not be given supplements and should be kept lean. With diligent testing and careful mating, the incidence in Pugs should improve."

Luxating Patella

A dog with a luxating patella experiences frequent dislocations of the kneecap. The condition is common in smaller breeds, and can affect one or both kneecaps. Surgery may be required to rectify the problem.

Often, owners have no idea anything is wrong with their dog's knee joint. Then the pet jumps off a bed or leaps to catch a toy, lands badly, and begins to limp and favor the other leg.

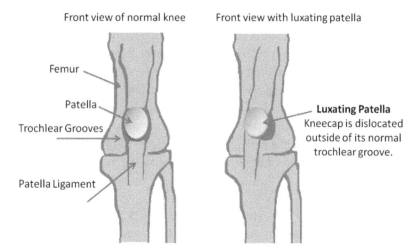

The condition may be genetic in origin, so it is important to ask a breeder if the problem has surfaced in the line of dogs he cultivates.

A luxating patella can also be the consequence of a physical injury, especially as a dog ages. For this reason, you want to discourage jumping in older dogs. Offer steps in key locations around the home to help your senior Pug navigate in safety.

Any time you see your dog limping or seeming more fatigued than usual after vigorous play, have the dog checked out. Conditions like a luxating patella only get worse with time and wear and need immediate treatment.

Classic signs are skipping as the patella luxates as they flex the stifle — this is the knee joint between the thigh bone (the femur) and the two lower leg bones (tibia and fibula).

Demodectic Mange

This skin disease often called Demodex is caused by parasitic mites (demodectic Mites). All dogs carry the Demodex mite as puppies pick them up from their mother. The mites live on your Pug's body all year round at the base of the fur follicles. Problems can occur when your Pug suffers from stress, malnutrition or has an underdeveloped or impaired immune system. At that point they are able to push out the hair and nip away at the skin.

You will start to notice small bald patches, often a reddish color, usually near the base of the ear opening, above the eyes, the belly and paws. Your Pug may also be lethargic and lose its appetite.

As long as your Pug does not have a genetic deficiency of its immune system, treatment of demodectic mange is usually successful although it can reoccur.

Hopefully demodectic mange is localized and only affecting a specific area of the body, because in 90% of these cases, the issue resolves itself naturally.

With generalized demodectic mange, symptoms will be more widespread and appear across the body and will require treatment, usually lime-sulfur insecticide dips to the affected areas, which helps relieve symptoms by killing the mites and their eggs.

Alternative treatments to the dippings (which can be traumatic) involve the use of antibiotics, topical solutions or shampoos designed for the treatment of this problem.

Follow-up checks will include skin scrapings, known as trichograms, which monitor the presence of mites and check the treatment's progress. With chronic long-term cases, regular medication may be necessary.

Pam Donaldson of Highland/Kendoric Pugs: "Any puppy that has generalized demodectic mange (covering large portions of the body) requiring medication and dips to clear it should NEVER be used in a breeding program as it is directly related to a compromised immune system. Unfortunately, dogs like these are used for breeding far too often by uneducated breeders."

The Matter of Genetic Abnormalities

Although responsible breeders work hard to eliminate potential genetic illnesses from their blood lines, there are some conditions for which no screening tests are available.

Also, Pugs that come from backyard breeders do not benefit from the same genetic cultivation and are even more susceptible to health issues. Before you adopt a Pug, you should be aware of the possibility of the following conditions, all of which are associated with the breed.

Pug Dog Encephalitis

The cause of Pug Dog Encephalitis (PDE) is unknown, but the condition occurs most often in dogs that are closely related. Researchers believe it is a hereditary immune-mediated disease. It is also known as Necrotizing Meningoencephalitis (NME). The Pug's immune system attacks normal brain tissue causing:

- changes in behavior
- stiffness of the neck with head tilt
- pressing of the head against objects and walls
- seizures
- poor coordination
- walking in circles
- confusion and disorientation
- depression and lethargy
- overall weakness
- blindness

PDE can manifest as early as six months of age, but is seen most often in dogs two to three years of age. Female, fawn-colored Pugs younger than seven are more likely to develop PDE/NME than older, male and non-fawn.

In many cases PDE strikes quickly, progresses rapidly, and leads to sudden death often during a seizure. In less severe cases, PDE can be controlled for a short period of time with anticonvulsant drugs. Unfortunately, PDE is always fatal. Contact your vet at the first sign of symptoms.

Brachycephalic Ocular Syndrome

Pugs, like all brachycephalic breeds, have large eyes that protrude. In dogs with excessively sagging lids that don't close completely, the corneas start to dry out.

The tear ducts can also become clogged and don't drain properly, causing constant tearing and staining. The eyes often become scratched, sometimes due to injury or to the presence of too many eyelashes, or those that are incorrectly placed.

The greatest potential for damage is to the cornea. Left untreated, even a minor scratch can progress to blindness as the eye begins to deposit the brown pigment melanin onto the cornea to make it tougher. Once in place, the melanin cannot be removed.

In Pugs with excessively bulging eyes, all of these problems come together to be described as a "syndrome." It may be necessary to administer lubricating eye drops and to maintain a constant vigil for potential injuries.

The eyes should be checked monthly to make sure there are no excess or oddly placed eyelashes. Monitor tear and mucus production and report anything to the vet that seems abnormal. Observe the cornea for any splotches that may be blue, white, or brown in color. Also watch the dog for squinting, which is a sign of pain.

Brachycephalic Obstructive Airway Syndrome (BOAS)

The Pug is a short-faced breed which puts it at risk for brachycephalic airway obstruction syndrome (also called brachycephalic respiratory syndrome). In layman's terms, abnormalities in the upper airways make it harder for the dog to inhale, leading the dog to breathe through its mouth rather than the nose.

In mild cases, the dog will exhibit noisy breathing when at play and make snorting sounds when excited. Expect a lot of snoring. In severe cases, the animal will tire out quickly and may even faint or collapse from the exertion. The symptoms will be worse in humid, hot weather.

Primary symptoms include:

- coughing
- gagging
- retching
- vomiting

Brachycephalic Airway Obstruction Syndrome is not actually a single disease, but a group of upper respiratory abnormalities which include everted laryngeal saccules, elongated soft palate, hypoplastic trachea, and stenotic nares. A dog with brachycephalic airway obstruction syndrome might have one, several, or all of these conditions.

Everted laryngeal saccules involve the small pouches in the larynx getting sucked into the airway during breathing, while elongated soft palate involves the soft tissue at the roof of the dog's mouth getting pulled into the airway.

Hypoplastic trachea refers to a trachea that is too narrow, while **stenotic nares** are nostrils that are too small. Any of these conditions can affect the dog's breathing, causing coughing or gagging as well as reduced tolerance to exercise and heat. Some of these conditions can be managed with corticosteroids or anti-inflammatories.

With hypoplastic tracheas, there is very little that can be done, however stenotic nares, elongated soft palates and everted laryngeal saccules can all be treated surgically. However, these are costly—for example, soft palate resection can cost from $500 to $1,500, while stenotic nares resection varies from $200 to $1,000.

Reverse sneezing is a phenomenon of the breed that can be very startling to the Pug guardian when they hear this snorting, gagging or honking sound for the first time. Often it is brought on when a dog becomes overly excited from quickly eating special treats, or when greeting another dog. Usually the dog will stop moving and hang its head during a reverse sneezing episode, and although it may be distressing to the dog, it is usually more distressing to the Pug owner.

There are several methods that can help overcome a reverse sneezing episode, including calming them, rubbing their nose so they open their mouth and begin breathing normally, and giving their chest a quick little squeeze on either side to force air out of their lungs. Sometimes, lightly blowing air into their face will also relieve the episode.

Most dogs will appear completely normal both before and after episodes of reverse sneezing and will continue to experience them intermittently throughout their lives.

Overheating can be a serious problem for dogs suffering from severe respiratory problems; the increased panting causes further swelling and narrowing of the airways, so don't exercise them in hot weather.

Sue Lee of Tsuselena Pugs: "The recent Vet Compass report and the Cambridge University BOAS team both identify obesity as the main reason Pug owners visit their vet and it is an important contributory factor for BOAS. The important message to Pug owners is to keep your Pug "Fit not Fat" and that stenotic nares can be an issue in cases of BOAS affected Pugs.

Christine Dresser DVM, Health Liaison, PDCA: "We had a veterinary surgeon, professor, author and Pug owner speak at our national. He said the major respiratory problem he sees, especially in middle-aged or older Pugs is laryngeal collapse. There is no surgery that will ameliorate this condition and it can only be managed with palliative care."

Portosystemic Shunt

The vascular anomaly called a portosystemic shunt diverts the flow of blood around the liver rather than into the organ. Consequently, the liver does not develop properly, and the blood is not filtered correctly.

The defect may be present at birth or develop later. The problem can be seen in any breed, but it is common in Pugs, Miniature Schnauzers, Cairn Terriers, Yorkshire Terriers, Scottish Terriers, Maltese, Golden Retrievers, Labrador Retrievers, Irish Wolfhounds, and Poodles.

Dogs with a portosystemic shunt develop poorly. The problem is often diagnosed when the dog is suffering from hepatic encephalopathy, which causes head pressing, swaying, an irregular gait, and seizures. The encephalopathy is caused by a buildup of toxins in the blood that then affect the brain.

Blood tests are used to diagnose the presence of a portosystemic shunt, which is then treated medically until the dog stabilizes and is then commonly followed by surgery. The dog will then need a low protein diet until the blood normalizes.

Christine Dresser DVM, Health Liaison, PDCA: "I have been lucky enough to discuss this problem at length with Dr. Sharon Center at Cornell who has spent a lifetime trying to unlock the genetics of this. From testing I have done, a large portion of Pugs will have slightly abnormal bile acids and upon liver biopsy, will have microvascular dysplasia, which is a sort of mild form of little shunts. These dogs are not clinical, have no disease and need no special treatment. However, if they are not tested as youngsters and develop health issues in later life, the mild elevations found when trying to find a cause for their health issue may be interpreted as being significant. Dr. Center also feels almost every dog can be managed medically and doesn't advocate going to surgery on most dogs."

Hemivertebrae

Brachycephalic breeds like the Pug often have a curled tail that may be a sign of a spinal abnormality called hemivertebrae. This is also seen in French and English Bulldogs and Boston Terriers.

If only the bones of the tail are affected, there is no major problem, but if the defect is in the backbone the animal may suffer pain, be more susceptible to injury, and have an overly arched back.

ymptoms are evident by the age of nine months when the spinal column is fully developed. Typically, two or more parts of the spinal column fail to fuse, causing compression. The dog's movement will be compromised often to the point of paralysis.

Weakness tends to appear first in the hind limbs. The dog will show a reluctance to move or to stand. The gait will become uncoordinated, and the dog may have difficulty passing urine and voiding feces.

In mild cases, corticosteroid injections help to relieve inflammation, but severe instances require spinal surgery to correct the deformity. Pain management and restricted activity are a vital part of treatment.

The prognosis varies by individual and clearly treatment is extremely expensive.

Pugs are like flowers they brighten your day

Photo Credit: Wendy Davenschot of Viking Mops, Pugtography.

Legg-Calve-Perthes Disease

Legg-Calve-Perthes Disease is a deformity of the ball of the hip joint. It is typically caused by some injury that prevents the head of the femur bone from receiving an adequate blood supply. Ultimately the bone collapses and the cartilage becomes deformed. Inflammation and arthritis then cause pain and lameness.

Symptoms include chewing at the flank region, general irritability, and progressive lameness. The muscles of the limb will atrophy, and the dog will experience pain when the hip moves.

Surgery to remove the femoral head and neck is a highly effective treatment although the dog may experience some residual lameness.

Entropion

Entropion is a condition in which the dog's eyelid turns inward, irritating the cornea. The issue becomes apparent in puppies with squinting and excessive tearing. In most cases, the condition resolves as the dog ages. Some dogs will have the condition and it will not improve with age and these dogs will require surgery.

In severe instances a canine ophthalmologist must tack the lids with stitches that will remain in place for a period of days or weeks until the correct "fit" is achieved. During healing, artificial tears are used to prevent drying of the eyes.

Distichiasis

A "distichia" is an eyelash that grows from an abnormal place on the eyelid or in an abnormal direction. This may occur on the upper or lower lid. Usually more than one is present; the plural is distichiae. This condition is similar to entropion.

If sufficiently severe, the abnormal eyelashes scratch the cornea causing ulceration. The eye and or conjunctiva may be red and inflamed.

Discharge can be present and the animal may blink excessively, squinting from pain, and keeping the eye closed. If ulceration has developed, the affected cornea will appear to be bluish. Mild cases may require no treatment, or the simple use of lubricating drops. Severe cases must be addressed with corrective surgery, but in such instances the prognosis is excellent.

Pigmentary Keratopathy

Pigmentary keratopathy/keratitis (PK) is a condition in which brown pigment progressively clouds the cornea (the clear tissue that allows light to enter the eye) and is a frequent cause of blindness in the Pug.

The cause of PK is not fully understood, but there is a strong correlation between genetic makeup, and trauma to the eye such as chronic irritation, corneal ulcers, or scarring.

No treatments are available to remove completely pigment that becomes established in the cornea as a result of PK although early detection and intervention can minimize the effects which is why I recommend a yearly examination by a veterinarian or veterinary ophthalmologist. Unfortunately many owners are not aware of the problem until it is too late to do anything about it.

Christine Dresser DVM, Health Liaison, PDCA: "83% of Pugs have it to varying degrees. Pigment can form on corneas due to trauma or scarring but the Pug pigment appears to be unique and breed specific. It is very discouraging for breeders as we don't know the genetics of it. One of my worst affected bitches has two offspring that are close to totally clear."

Pug Myelopathy

This spinal condition is considered the most frequent cause of rear limb incoordination (ataxia) and is a progressive weakness, resulting in staggering in the rear legs of middle-aged to older Pugs, and often includes fecal and/or urinary incontinence. In a period of one to four years it can even lead to paralysis of the rear limbs.

Believed to be unique in Pugs, little is known about it and there is no consensus among neurologists about the best way to treat it. Surgery may be appropriate for individual cases, but it must be considered as soon as possible after symptoms first occur and may only delay the progression of paralysis. However, Pugs affected with Myelopathy are usually pain free and can lead excellent long lives with good nursing care.

Chapter 12 — Helping Your Senior Pug Live Longer

Obviously it can be incredibly sad to see your beloved Pug grow older. Unfortunately, aging is a natural part of life that cannot be avoided. All you can do is to learn how to provide for your Pug's needs as he ages so you can keep him with you for as long as possible.

He may develop health problems like arthritis, and he simply might not be as active as he once was. You are likely to notice a combination of both physical and mental (behavior) changes, as body and mind start to slow. However, with good veterinary care and proper nutrition, he can live for many years and you can help extend his life.

Elderly Pugs and What to Expect

Aging is a natural part of life for both humans and dogs. Sadly, dogs reach the end of their lives sooner than most humans. Once your Pug reaches the age of eight years or so, he can be considered a "senior" dog. At this point, you may need to start feeding him a dog food specially formulated for older dogs.

Because their **metabolism slows down**, they will put on weight unless their daily calories are reduced. Unfortunately, this weight then places extra stress on their joints and organs, making them work harder than before.

In order to properly care for your Pug as he ages, you might find it helpful to know what to expect as your dog starts to get older:

1. Your Pug's **joints** may start to give him trouble—check for swelling and signs of stiffness, often due to arthritis, and consult your veterinarian with any problems.

2. Your dog may be **less active** than he was in his youth he will likely still enjoy walks, but he may not last as long as he once did, and he might take it at a slower pace.

3. Organs, such as heart or liver, may not function as effectively.

4. He may have an occasional "accident" inside the house as a result of incontinence. He may also urinate more frequently.

5. Your Pug may **sleep more** than he once did—this is a natural sign of aging, but it can also be a symptom of a health problem, so consult your vet if his sleeping becomes excessive.

6. He may have a greater tendency to **gain weight**, so you will need to carefully monitor his diet to keep him from becoming obese in his old age.

7. Brain activity is affected—your Pug's **memory**, ability to learn, and awareness will all start to weaken. He may wander round aimlessly or fail to respond to basic commands.

8. He may have **trouble walking** or jumping, so keep an eye on your Pug if he has difficulty jumping, or if he starts dragging his back feet.

9. You may need to trim your Pug's nails more frequently if he doesn't spend as much time outside as he once did when he was younger.

10. Your Pug will develop gray hair around the face and muzzle—this may be less noticeable in Pugs with a lighter coat.

11. Your Pug's **vision** may deteriorate. Be careful if his eyes appear cloudy. This could be a sign of cataracts, and you should see your vet as soon as you notice this.

12. He may develop halitosis (bad breath), which can be a sign of dental or gum disease. Get this checked out by a vet.

13. He may also become more protective of you around strangers, be increasingly irritable, and bark and whine more.

While many of the signs mentioned above are natural side effects of aging, they can also be symptoms of serious health conditions. If your Pug develops any of these problems suddenly, consult your veterinarian immediately.

Vallarie Smith Cuttie of Peachtree Pugs: "I have always heard that a Pug's life expectancy is about 10-14 years, and in my experience (first Pug in 1991) I think this is about right. My first Pug, Fife, lived to be 15.5 and my sweet old Gumbo (CH Peachtree's I Will Play For Gumbo) lived to the ripe old age of 16.5! When he got old we took a picture of him every birthday in his party hat with the new number on it ... he

was such a dear, sweet, old man and although he died several years ago we miss him so very much."

"When asked how to increase the probability of a great long life I tell people to love their Pugs extremely well. Keep them well fed on premium dog food, no table scraps, and keep their weight normal. Fresh water should be available to them at all times. Keep them loved and stimulated with lots of companionship with humans and other dogs, lots of naps when needed and plenty of lap time in the evenings. I stress that people NOT over-vaccinate their Pugs and that they never hesitate to get them to the vet when they aren't well. It NEVER fails, Pugs will return your love tenfold every day!"

Photo Credit: Julianne McCoy of Low Country Pugs.

Julianne McCoy of Low Country Pugs: "Giving dental bones or using some other method for cleaning teeth can allow a Pug to age without losing their teeth. I have a 15 year old Pug that just has a little arthritis and she has all of her teeth. Of course she is almost blind. I have to clap my hands so that she knows where I am so she can still function as she has. She is an independent old Pug."

Thirteen Tips for Caring for Pugs in Old Age

When your Pug gets older, he may require different care than he did when he was younger. The more you know about what to expect as your Pug ages, the better equipped you will be to provide him with the care he needs to remain healthy and mobile.

1. Supplement your dog's diet with DHA and EPA fatty acids to help prevent joint stiffness and arthritis.

2. Schedule routine annual visits with your veterinarian to make sure your Pug is in good condition.

3. Consider switching to a dog food that is specially formulated for senior/mature dogs—a food that is too high in calories may cause your dog to gain weight. Some are labeled as from age eight, others for even older dogs such as 10+. Take it **slowly** when switching to minimize the impact on their digestive system, which cannot cope with sudden change.

4. Brush his teeth regularly to prevent periodontal diseases, which are fairly common in older dogs. A daily dental stick helps reduce tartar, freshen breath, and improve gum health.

5. Continue to exercise your Pug on a regular basis—he may not be able to move as quickly, but you still need to keep him active to maintain joints, muscle health, and vital organs such as heart, lungs, and joints.

6. Provide your Pug with **soft bedding** on which to sleep. Put down carpet or rugs on hard floors—slippery hardwood or tile flooring can be very problematic for arthritic dogs.

7. Ensure his usual environment is not too noisy, as he will need to rest and sleep more to recharge his body. Make sure it is neither too hot nor cold, as his body **may not regulate** his temperature as well as it used to.

8. Keep your Pug's **mind exercised** as well as his body. Playing games and introducing new toys will achieve this.

9. Use **ramps** to get your dog into the car and onto the bed (if he is allowed), because he may no longer be able to jump.

10. Avoid **sugar and grains** which can be acid-forming and pro-inflammatory, as well as being an unnatural food for dogs.

11. Cat's claw is a Peruvian vine available in dry powder, tea, tincture and supplement form that has anti-inflammatory properties and is used for relief from arthritic pain.

12. For rebuilding muscles, skin, cartilage, tendons and ligaments, a good dietary source of vitamin C is necessary, together with an organic form of Sulphur (it is a component of collagen).

13. Homoeopathic remedies can help with pain and inflammation too—arnica can help reduce bruising of tissues.

The most important thing you can do for your senior dog is to schedule regular visits with your veterinarian. However, you should also keep an eye out for signs of disease as your dog ages. If you notice your elderly Pug exhibiting any of the following symptoms, you would be wise to seek veterinary care for your dog as soon as possible:

• Decreased appetite
• Increased thirst and urination
• Difficulty urinating/constipation
• Blood in the urine
• Difficulty breathing/coughing
• Vomiting or diarrhea
• Poor coat condition

Why I Recommend Pet Insurance

I believe in preventive maintenance as much as possible. My own dogs are seen by a veterinary chiropractor fairly regularly from the time they are about nine weeks old, and they are well-exercised to avoid the "weekend athlete" injuries. I have been blessed with overall sound and healthy Pugs, but nevertheless I wouldn't be without my pet health insurance just in case the worst happens.

Thanks to advances in veterinary science, our pets now receive viable and effective treatments. The estimated annual cost for a medium-sized dog, including healthcare, is about $650 / £400 (this does not include emergency care, advanced procedures, or consultations with specialists.) The growing interest in pet insurance to help defray these costs is understandable. You can buy a policy covering accidents, illness, and hereditary and chronic conditions for about $25 / £16.25 per month. Benefit caps and deductibles vary by company.

A good policy should have lifetime coverage, not 12 months only, and checking the small print for the level of coverage is worthwhile, as you really do get what you pay for.

Although breeders are striving to improve the overall health of the Pug, it is inevitable that you will need to make a number of visits to the vet in your Pug's lifetime. Apart from the routine of annual injections and check-ups, there are bound to be unexpected visits, often at weekends or in the middle of the night, when costs are significantly higher. This total can run to thousands of dollars (or pounds).

I know from my vet friends that they feel frustrated knowing the owner cares and would like to do everything possible, but the finances are not always available. Make sure you either insure your dog well or have a savings pot available for any unexpected expenses. Visits to referral specialists can allow many amazing things to be done, but expect to pay a few thousand dollars or pounds for the privilege of such up-to-date care. Pugs can live well into their teens, but this means senior costs such as arthritis medication, so make sure you can provide everything you would like to keep your old friend happy and healthy.

Establishing a healthy record from the very beginning ensures your Pug qualifies for full insurance coverage and lower premiums. To get rate quotes, investigate the following companies:

United States

http://www.24PetWatch.com
http://www.ASPCAPetInsurance.com
http://www.PetsBest.com
http://www.PetInsurance.com

United Kingdom

http://www.Animalfriends.org.uk

http://www.Healthy-pets.co.uk
http://www.Petplan.co.uk

Grieving a Lost Pet

The hardest decision any pet owner makes is helping a suffering animal to pass easily and humanely. I have been in this position. Even though I know my beloved companions died peacefully and with no pain, my own anguish was considerable. Thankfully, I was in the care of, and accepted the advice and counsel of, exceptional veterinary professionals.

This is the crucial component in the decision to euthanize an animal. For your own peace of mind, you must know that you have the best medical advice possible. My vet was not only knowledgeable and patient, but she was kind and forthright. I valued those qualities and hope you are as blessed as I was in the same situation.

It is heartbreaking for any Pug owner to know that it is time to say goodbye to their beloved pet. But how does one know when the time is right? Many people think that their dog will "let them know" when the time has come. I came to believe that **we owe our Pugs the best life** that we can provide for them. When they have been a part of your life for 12–15 years, you can see when things change drastically enough to have to make that difficult decision.

I started a calendar with my boy when it was obvious time was running out. Every day I would make a notation. Good day/bad day. When the bad days outweighed the good days, I made the decision to let my dog pass. A wise person once told me, "Better a day too soon, than a day too late." Our pets rely on us to make that decision for them. Make sure you have a vet that is sensitive to your feelings and will provide you with the time to spend with your dog to say goodbye. Euthanasia is the last kind gift we can give to that special dog."

The bottom line is that you must make the best decision that you can for your pet, and for yourself. So long as you are acting from a position of love, respect, and responsibility, whatever you do is "right."

Some humans have difficulty fully recognizing the terrible grief involved in losing a beloved canine friend. There will be many who **do not understand** the close bond we humans can have with our dogs, which is often unlike any we have with our human counterparts.

Your friends may give you pitying looks and try to cheer you up, but if they have never experienced the loss of such a special connection themselves, they may also secretly think you are making too much fuss over "just a dog." For some of us humans, the loss of a beloved dog is so painful that we decide never to share our lives with another, because the thought of going through the pain of such a loss is unbearable.

Expect to feel terribly sad, tearful, and yes, depressed, because those who are close to their canine companions will feel their loss no less acutely than the loss of a human friend or life partner. The grieving process can take some time to recover from, and some of us never totally recover.

After the loss of a family dog, first you need to take care of yourself by making certain that you remember to eat regular meals and get enough sleep, even though you will feel an almost eerie sense of loneliness.

Losing a beloved dog is a shock to the system that can also affect your concentration and your ability to find joy or be interested in participating in other activities that are a normal part of your daily life.

Other dogs, cats, and pets in the home will also be grieving the loss of a companion and may display this by acting depressed, being off their food, or showing little interest in play or games. Therefore, you need to help guide your other pets through this grieving process by keeping them busy and interested, taking them for extra walks, and finding ways to spend more time with them.

Wait Long Enough

Many people **do not wait long enough** before attempting to replace a lost pet and will immediately go to the local shelter and rescue a deserving dog. While this may help to distract you from your grieving process, this is not really fair to the new furry member of your family.

Bringing a new pet into a home that is depressed and grieving the loss of a long-time canine member may create behavioral problems for the new dog that will be faced with learning all about their new home, while also dealing with the unstable energy of the grieving family.

A better scenario would be to **allow yourself the time to properly grieve** by waiting a minimum of one month to give yourself and your family time to feel happier and more stable before deciding upon sharing your home with another dog.

Afterword

Getting to know my first Pug in the company of a human with mobility challenges—a guy who really wanted and needed a companion animal—was a great experience. It gave me a real appreciation for the Pug's sterling qualities even in the face of what is arguably a great deal of maintenance.

If I had simply read that this is a breed that takes six months to housebreak, has an unbelievable urge to chew as a puppy, and sheds like a demon year round for life, I might have formed a completely different opinion of the Pug.

Instead, I saw how Bentley, a little comedian on four paws, made my friend Mike laugh. Mike survived a horrible car accident as a young man that left him partially crippled and in chronic pain. He was fortunate to be able to work from home, but there were a lot of long hours in his day that Bentley made better.

After Bentley passed, Mike adopted a second Pug and they have developed an equally strong bond. Mike freely admits that he is completely spoiled for any other breed. Even if he does have to wipe his dog's facial wrinkles every day and clean up the occasional puddle when the Pug refuses to go outside when it's raining, he has a good-humored companion with low exercise needs that makes him laugh.

While the Pug may not be the dog for everyone, they are an exceptional breed that does well in virtually any residential setting. They get along well with other pets and are truly fond of children, so the Pug is an excellent choice as a family dog.

Additionally, with an expected lifespan of 15 years, you stand a good chance of having your Pug with you a very long time. In general this is a hardy breed, and so long as you adopt from a reputable breeder that closely monitors its bloodlines, you should not be faced with any of the genetic illnesses associated with Pugs.

If you do decide to bring a Pug into your home, be prepared to meet a "multum in parvo" —a big dog in a little body!

The bottom line in any purchase is to consider the needs of the animal first and then to evaluate the fit with your lifestyle. If his life won't work with yours, admire him from afar, as nothing else is fair to a dog

of the Pug's unmistakable and unique quality.

If, however, the Pug is the right dog for you, he's an affectionate, loyal, smart little hound with a unique take on the world and you can't beat owning this incredible dog.

Photo Credit: Julie Squire & Holly Attwood of Taftazini.

Laura Libner of Lorarlar Pugs adds: "I think, for me, what endears me so much to the Pug breed is their sweet, silly personality and ability to be as exuberant about seeing me whether I'm gone for an hour, or a week. They are a breed that brims over with joy and silly capers/antics and are always surprising me with cute little nuances of their individual personalities. They look at you and you know if they are happy, sad, not feeling well, etc. A breed of dog that is easy to understand, very companionable ... and also very vulnerable because of the overall conformation."

Jade Hall of SmugPugs: "The Pug is a natural clown—more like a human toddler in a fur coat than a dog. They watch TV, open gates and cupboards, and their main goal in life is to be close to their human. They're happy, funny, loving little souls whose only job is to be a companion."

Connie J. Dunham of MtnAire Pugs also tells us why you might choose a Pug: "In our modern world, many people don't have the space to adequately care for a large dog. Pugs fill a big gap between small dogs that look and act small, and large dogs who don't fit on a lap! Pugs are the largest of the toy breeds and are very substantial. They fare well with small children's antics while also not overpowering them. They love attention and just want to be with their people. While not likely to be found with a man in the hunting field, Pugs love walks and activities, riding in four-wheelers and pickups, and joining in a sledding party. Men can be their buddies as well as women. Their smallness makes them great for apartments and for lap companions for the elderly.

"I have always thought that looking into the face of a Pug is not like looking at a dog. They connect with you in a personal way, and have a special sense of understanding their people. One of my Pugs had special connections with my horses and cats, and any visiting dogs were mesmerized by her! Pugs don't have a loud, sharp bark and usually only make noise when visitors first arrive, so they work well with neighbors close by. They are not nervous or flighty and perform their comical routines just to help you get through a crazy day! Their purpose in life is to entertain you and love you. What else could you ask for in a little furry companion?"

SURPRISE — FREE BONUS PUG BOOK!

I want to say thank you for purchasing this book and to give you a special surprise. To show my appreciation I have compiled extra material that we just didn't have space for in this book, into a **free e-book that you can download.**

This gives you even more value by giving you free access to some exclusive bonus interviews with our expert Pug breeders. It contains more of an insight into some of the breeders who were actively involved in the making of this book. You will find some cute and funny stories about our loveable Pugs as well as even more tips and advice.

I would also really appreciate it if you could leave a positive review on the website where you bought this book. The more excellent 5-star reviews the book receives, the higher it will appear in the charts. We would really love to get this book out to as many Pug owners as possible.

If you have any comments to help us improve the book, then I would love to hear them personally and we can then revise the book as necessary. This is far more constructive than leaving a harmful review.

Thank you once again. To get the free book, just go to the web page below and follow the instructions. If you have any issues or feedback/ comments, please send an email to sales@dogexperts.info

GET THE FREE BONUS INTERVIEWS...

Go to this exclusive (and secret) webpage to download your free bonus book gift:

https://www.dogexperts.info/pug/gift/

Appendix — The Pug Breed Standard

The breed standard provides the main blueprint for a number of dog attributes that include a dog breed's physical appearance, his unique moves, and the type of temperament that each breed is expected to have. Created and laid down by the breed societies, dogs that are purebred (pedigree) have their registrations kept by the American Kennel Club (AKC) and the Kennel Club (in the UK).

Breeders approved by these Kennel Clubs have consented to breed puppies based on strict standards of breeding. They do not just simply mate any available male or female (sire or dam)! Also Pugs that are in shows run under AKC and Kennel Club rules are judged against the ideal list of attributes as laid out in the breed standard.

Photo Credit: Hilary Linnett of Conquell Pugs.

In the USA the Pug has been categorized into the toy group of breeds which also includes the Cavalier King Charles Spaniel, Chihuahua, Havanese, Maltese, Shih Tzu, Pekingese and Yorkshire Terrier.

The AKC describe the characteristics of the toy group as follows: "The diminutive size and winsome expressions of Toy dogs illustrate the main function of this Group: to embody sheer delight. Don't let their tiny stature fool you, though—many Toys are tough as nails. If you haven't yet experienced the barking of an angry Chihuahua, for example, well, just wait. Toy dogs will always be popular with city dwellers and people without much living space. They make ideal apartment dogs and terrific lap warmers on nippy nights. (Incidentally, small breeds may be found in every Group, not just the Toy Group. We advise everyone to seriously consider getting a small breed, when appropriate, if for no other reason than to minimize some of the problems inherent in canines such as shedding, creating messes and cost of care. And training aside, it's still easier to control a ten-pound dog than it is one ten times that size.)"

The following breed standard was approved by the American Kennel Club in 1957. It is reproduced verbatim here for reference purposes. The only changes incorporated are typographical to enhance readability.

AKC Official Standard of the Pug

General Appearance: Symmetry and general appearance are decidedly square and cobby. A lean, leggy Pug and a dog with short legs and a long body are equally objectionable.

Size, Proportion, Substance: The Pug should be "multum in parvo", and this condensation (if the word may be used) is shown by compactness of form, well-knit proportions, and hardness of developed muscle: Weight from 14 to 18 pounds (dog or bitch) desirable. Proportion: square.

Head: The head is large, massive, round - not apple-headed, with no indentation of the skull. The eyes are dark in color, very large, bold and prominent, globular in shape, soft and solicitous in expression, very lustrous, and, when excited, full of fire. The ears are thin, small, soft, like black velvet. There are two kinds - the "rose" and the "button." Preference is given to the latter. The wrinkles are large and deep. The muzzle is short, blunt, square, but not upfaced. Bite—a Pug's bite should be very slightly undershot.

Neck, Topline, Body: The neck is slightly arched. It is strong, thick, and with enough length to carry the head proudly. The short back is level rom the withers to the high tail set. The body is short and cobby, wide n chest and well ribbed up. The tail is curled as tightly as possible over he hip. The double curl is perfection.

orequarters: The legs are very strong, straight, of moderate length, nd are set well under. The elbows should be directly under the withers vhen viewed from the side. The shoulders are moderately laid back. The pasterns are strong, neither steep nor down. The feet are neither so ong as the foot of the hare, nor so round as that of the cat; well split-up oes, and the nails black. Dewclaws are generally removed.

Hindquarters: The strong, powerful hindquarters have moderate bend of stifle and short hocks perpendicular to the ground. The legs are parallel when viewed from behind. The hindquarters are in balance vith the forequarters. The thighs and buttocks are full and muscular: feet as in front.

Coat: The coat is fine, smooth, soft, short and glossy, neither hard nor woolly.

Color: The colors are fawn or black. The fawn color should be decided so as to make the contrast complete between the color and the trace and mask.

Markings: The markings are clearly defined. The muzzle or mask, ears, moles on cheeks, thumb mark or diamond on forehead, and the back trace should be as black as possible. The mask should be black. The more intense and well defined it is, the better. The trace is a black line extending from the occiput to the tail.

Gait: Viewed from the front, the forelegs should be carried well forward, showing no weakness in the pasterns, the paws landing squarely with the central toes straight ahead. The rear action should be strong and free through hocks and stifles, with no twisting or turning in or out at the joints. The hind legs should follow in line with the front. There is a slight natural convergence of the limbs both fore and aft. A slight roll of the hindquarters typifies the gait which should be free, self-assured, and jaunty.

Temperament: This is an even-tempered breed, exhibiting stability, playfulness, great charm, dignity, and an outgoing, loving disposition.

Disqualification: Any color other than fawn or black.

UK Kennel Club Official Standard for the Pug

The UK Kennel Club has placed the Pug in the toy category. They say: "Toy breeds are small companion or lapdogs. Many of the Toy breeds were bred for this capacity although some have been placed into this category simply due to their size. They should have friendly personalities and love attention. They do not need a large amount of exercise and some can be finicky eaters."

The following standard was approved by The Kennel Club in July 2017. It is reproduced verbatim here for reference purposes. The only changes incorporated are typographical to enhance readability.

General Appearance: Decidedly square and cobby, it is "multum in parvo" shown in compactness of form, well-knit proportions and hardness of muscle, but never to appear low on legs, nor lean and leggy.

Characteristics: Great charm, dignity and intelligence.

Temperament: Even-tempered, happy and lively disposition.

Head and Skull: Head relatively large and in proportion to body, round, not apple-headed, with no indentation of skull. Muzzle relatively short, blunt, square, not upfaced. Nose black, fairly large with wide, open nostrils. Wrinkles on forehead clearly defined without exaggeration. Eyes or nose never adversely affected or obscured by over nose wrinkle. Pinched nostrils and heavy over nose wrinkle is unacceptable and should be heavily penalised.

Eyes: Dark, relatively large, round in shape, soft and solicitous in expression, very lustrous, and when excited, full of fire. Never protruding, exaggerated or showing white when looking straight ahead. Free from obvious eye problems.

Ears: Thin, small, soft like black velvet. Two kinds: 'Button ear' – ear flap folding forward, tip lying close to skull to cover opening. 'Rose ear' – small drop ear which folds over and back to reveal the burr.

Mouth: Slightly undershot. Wide lower jaw with incisors almost in a straight line. Wry mouths, teeth or tongue showing all highly undesirable and should be heavily penalised.

Neck: Slightly arched to resemble a crest, strong, thick with enough length to carry head proudly.

Forequarters: Legs very strong, straight, of moderate length, and well under body. Shoulders well sloped.

Body: Short and cobby, broad in chest. Ribs well sprung and carried well back. Topline level neither roached nor dipping.

Hindquarters: Legs very strong, of moderate length, with good turn of stifle, well under body, straight and parallel when viewed from rear.

Feet: Neither so long as the foot of the hare, not so round as that of the cat; well split-up toes; the nails black.

Tail: High-set, tightly curled over hip. Double curl highly desirable.

Gait/Movement: Viewed from in front should rise and fall with legs well under shoulder, feet keeping directly to front, not turning in or out. From behind, action just as true. Using forelegs strongly putting them well forward with hind legs moving freely and using stifles well. A slight, unexaggerated roll of hindquarters typifies gait. Capable of purposeful and steady movement.

Coat: Fine, smooth, soft, short and glossy, neither harsh, off-standing nor woolly. Any stripping or trimming of the coat which alters the length, texture or outline must be penalised.

Colour: Silver, apricot, fawn or black. Each clearly defined, to make contrast complete between colour, trace (black line extending from occiput to tail) and mask. Markings clearly defined. Muzzle or mask, ears, moles on cheeks, thumb mark or diamond on forehead and trace as black as possible.

Size: Ideal weight 6.3 – 8.1 kg. (14–18 lb.). Should be hard of muscle but substance must not be confused with overweight.

Faults: Any departure from the foregoing points should be considered a fault and the seriousness with which the fault should be regarded should be in exact proportion to its degree.

NOTE: Male animals should have two apparently normal testicles fully descended into the scrotum.

Glossary—Unusual Terms Demystified!

Abdomen — The surface area of a dog's body lying between the chest and the hindquarters also referred to as the belly.

Allergy — An abnormally sensitive reaction to substances including pollens, foods, or microorganisms. May be present in humans or animals with similar symptoms including, but not limited to, sneezing, itching, and skin rashes.

Anal glands — Glands located on either side of a dog's anus used to mark territory. May become blocked and require treatment by a veterinarian.

Arm — On a dog, the region between the shoulder and the elbow is referred to as the arm or the upper arm.

Back — That portion of a dog's body that extends from the withers (or shoulder) to the croup (approximately the area where the back flows into the tail.)

Bitch — The appropriate term for a female dog.

Blooded — An accepted reference to a pedigreed dog.

Breed — A line or race of dogs selected and cultivated by man from a common gene pool to achieve and maintain a characteristic appearance and function.

Breed standard — A written "picture" of a perfect specimen of a given breed in terms of appearance, movement, and behavior as formulated by a parent organization, for example, the American Kennel Club or in Great Britain, The Kennel Club.

Brows — The contours of the frontal bone that form ridges above a dog's eyes.

Buttocks — The hips or rump of a dog.

Castrate — The process of removing a male dog's testicles.

Chest — That portion of a dog's trunk or body encased by the ribs.

Coat — The hair covering a dog. Most breeds have both an outer coat and an undercoat.

Cobby — Having short legs and a compact body; stocky.

Come into Season — The point at which a female dog becomes fertile for purposes of mating.

Congenital — Any quality, particularly an abnormality, present at birth.

Crate — Any portable container used to house a dog for transport or provided to a dog in the home as a "den."

Crossbred — Dogs are said to be crossbred when each of their parents is of a different breed.

Dam — A term for the female parent.

Dew Claw — Can be compared to the equivalent of a human thumb. In dogs, over time this has moved over time to a position up the inside of the front leg and is now a functionless digit often removed in puppies to prevent possible injuries.

Euthanize—The act of relieving the suffering of a terminally ill animal by inducing a humane death, typically with an overdose of anesthesia.

Fancier — Any person with an exceptional interest in purebred dogs and the shows where they are exhibited.

Groom — To make a dog's coat neat by brushing, combing, or trimming.

Harness — A cloth or leather strap shaped to fit the shoulders and chest of a dog with a ring at the top for attaching a lead. An alternative to using a collar.

Haunch Bones — Terminology for the hip bones of a dog.

Haw — The membrane inside the corner of a dog's eye known as the third eyelid.

Head — The cranium and muzzle of a dog.

Hip Dysplasia — A condition in dogs due to a malformation of the hip resulting in painful and limited movement of varying degrees.

Hindquarters — The back portion of a dog's body including the pelvis, thighs, hocks, and paws.

Hock — Bones on the hind leg of a dog that form the joint between the second thigh and the metatarsus. Known as the dog's true heel.

Lead — Any strap, cord, or chain used to restrain or lead a dog. Typically attached to a collar or harness. Also called a leash.

Litter — The puppy or puppies from a single birth or "whelping."

Mask — The black skin pigmentation and hairs on the face which is part of what sets this breed aside and lends to its amazing appearance. It begins under the chin and covers the entire muzzle, raising over the top of the nose and encircling both eyes.

Multum in parvo — Latin expression that has so appropriately become the motto of the Pug. It literally means, "Much in little."

Muzzle — That portion of a dog's head lying in front of the eyes and consisting of the nasal bone, nostrils, and jaws.

Neuter — To castrate or spay a dog thus rendering them incapable of reproducing.

Pastern — The front pastern is the dogs' main shock absorber between the knee and the paw.

Pedigree — The written record of a pedigreed dog's genealogy. Should extend to three or more generations.

Puppy — Any dog of less than 12 months of age.

Roach — An arched back.

Separation Anxiety — The anxiety and stress suffered by a dog left alone for any period of time.

Sire — The accepted term for the male parent.

Spay — The surgery to remove a female dog's ovaries to prevent conception.

Stifle — Equivalent of the human knee. The stifle joint joins three bones: the femur, patella, and tibia.

Stop — The skull ends at the stop. The area called the 'stop' begins where the brows or frontal bones surround the eyes, and ends at the muzzle.

Whelping — Term for the act of giving birth to puppies.

Withers — The highest point of a dog's shoulders.

Relevant Websites

American Kennel Club
http://www.akc.org/

The Kennel Club - UK
http://www.thekennelclub.org.uk

Pug Dog Club of America
http://www.pugdogclubofamerica.com/

Pug Dog Club UK
http://www.pugdogclub.org.uk

Pug Club of Canada
http://www.pugcanada.com/

Pug Breed Council (UK)
https://pugbreedcouncil.wordpress.com/

Pug Health (UK)
http://www.pughealth.org.uk/

Pug Rescue of North Carolina Inc
http://www.pugrescuenc.org/

Australian National Kennel Council
http://ankc.org.au/

Pug Club of Victoria Inc (Australia)
http://www.pugclubofvictoria.com.au/

The Pug Dog Club of NSW Inc (Australia)
http://www.pugclubofnsw.com/

The Pug Dog Welfare & Rescue Association (UK)
http://pugwelfare-rescue.org.uk/

Lightning Source UK Ltd.
Milton Keynes UK
UKHW021317190319
339444UK00009B/349/P